PSYCHOLOGY OF ADOLESCENTS IN INDIA

PROF. S. P. CHAUBE
M.A., M.Ed. (Alld.),
D.Ed. (Indiana, U.S.A.),
D. Litt. (Lucknow),
Recipient of the G.J. Watumull
Memorial Award in Education.
Retired : Dean & Professor of Education,
University of Gorakhpur (U.P.)

CONCEPT PUBLISHING COMPANY, NEW DELHI - 110059

ISBN 91-7022-913-8 (HB)

First Published 2002

Published and Printed by
Ashok Kumar Mittal
Concept Publishing Company
A/15-16, Commercial Block, Mohan Garden
NEW DELHI-110 059

Phones : 5648039, 5649024
Fax : 091-11-5648053
Email : publishing@conceptpub.com

Preface

Adolescence is a period of life in which many such changes take place which revolutionalise one's physical, emotional, mental and social settings. These changes are so all-pervasive and effective that the total outlook of an individual is modified, transformed and altered. An adolescent wants to be recognised as a full member of society having a unique personality of his own. He feels tempted to express his opinion on an issue without being asked for the same, but proper attention is never given to what he says. The adolescent, sometimes, faces great difficulties when he finds that the parents and other elders at home and teachers at school are in no way prepared to slacken their strict control over him. This is so because they regard him still as a child unmindful of the intricacies of his surroundings. The main intention of elders are generally to mould the future of the adolescent according to their own idiosyncrasies which the adolescent vehemently resents. Consequently, the adolescent very often thinks of throwing off the yoke of control imposed on him by elders. He experiences great stress and strain, because he wants to follow the path of his life according to his own inclinations and attitudes. The purpose of this book is to make the elders aware of the great mental and emotional ups and downs under which the adolescent, generally, seethes at times when he is hounded by elders. There is no doubt that the elders always cherish the good of their adolescent wards, but an obstacle crops in when they are after imposition of their own ways against the unwilling adolescents. This situation creates a difficult situation both for the adolescents and the elders. This book throws light on the various riddles in which an adolescent happens to be engrossed in from time to time as long as he remains under the strict control of his elders.

Keeping in view of the difficult situation of an adolescent we have cautioned parents and teachers in this book to be more psychological and sympathetic in their dealings with adolescents, if they want to let them grow in a manner which is individually satisfying and socially desirable. About an adolescent an elder encounters many such junctures wherein he (elder) gets non-plussed and does not understand how to come out of the lybrinth that he himself has engineered by his unpsychological behaviours. We have deliberately drawn the attention of readers to such points with a view to offer some positive suggestions to be followed by parents and teachers in relation to adolescents if the latter's healthy growth is to be ensured.

In view of the various facets of behaviours of adolescents, we have chosen to discuss in this book the significance of puberty and the allied physical changes which propel various types of emotional behaviours of adolescents. Personal, social and recreational interests cropping up from the many-sided growth of adolescents have also been projected out at relevant places throughout the book. Nature of friendship, feeling of sex and difficulties of newly married adolescent couples have been analysed for helping the all concerned for developing the appropriate mental attitude regarding the same. Religious doubts as harboured at times by some adolescents alongwith their developing sense of morality in Indian adolescents have also been given a place in preparation of this book. Towards the close of the book we have further emphasised the need of suitable guidance that our adolescents need so badly.

The author hopes that the aforementioned aspects will help the parents at home and teachers at schools to understand the naturalness of adolescents' behaviours in various situations of their normal development. It is the reader to judge the extent to which the author has succeeded in his attempts herein. Nevertheless, he will feel amply rewarded if this attempt on his part helps a reader to understand an adolescent under his care in a more psychological manner.

In a way, it will be preposterous on the part of the author to claim any kind of originality in a book of this nature. However, certain critical observations made at relevant places in this book for attracting the attention of parents and teachers with regard to their ways of dealing with adolescents have been his own. It is at such places alone that the author may claim some marks of originality. It is hoped that these marks will merit the attention of the readers.

The author very much hopes that this book will be interesting and helpful also to all graduate and post-graduate students of "Psychology" and 'Education', as the subject-matter herein treated appears to be quite relevant to some aspects of their curricular demands both in "psychology" and "Education".

S.P. CHAUBE

Karma Bhumi,
B-955, Sector A,
Near New Railway Crossing,
Mahanagar, Lucknow-226 006, (U.P.)

Contents

1

Introduction

Adolescence in human life is the stage when rapid changes take place. The individual's physical, mental, social, moral and spiritual outlooks undergo revolutionary changes. Such changes during adolescence are more rapid than during infancy or childhood. Due to this growth human personality develops new dimensions. Many parents fail to assess these changes and generally show indifference because they do not like to slacken their control over their children. This attitude creates many difficulties for the adolescent. During adolescence the individual wants to take independent decisions in various situations of his experiences. This is regarded by the elders as an act of indiscipline or of misconduct. Gradually, the adolescent starts to control his desire according to standards set by the society. He also begins to realise his social responsibilities. If he fails in this attempt, he develops many defects in his personality. We shall try to understand all these in this book.

Changes during Adolescence Quite Natural

Adolescence is a very important period of one's life. Revolutionary changes in one's experiences and character begin from the very beginning of this stage. The adolescent wants to give up many old things and habits of childhood and wants to acquire new ideas and habits in their place. In fact, he develops a tendency to learn new modes of behaviour. He now realises better as to what is good or bad for him. His mental faculties become more alert. Gradually he develops a new character and personality. People now believe that due to this tendency many ills in the child will disappear automatically when he enters adolescence. For instance, the weak child becomes stronger, the selfish one becomes more liberal, the short-tempered

---

Note : The use of the pronoun "he" in this book stands for the common gender.

develops some tolerance, the dirty boy starts observing cleanliness and the dull-headed becomes more intelligent and so on. People begin to think so about adolescence. Psychologists also confirm this thinking to some extent. However, it will be wrong to think that the individual gives up all his undesirable habits and activities during adolescence. There is no doubt that with more intelligence and experience the adolescent's understanding of things develops, but this understanding may be both in the right or wrong direction. The environment influences this understanding to a great extent. Some scientific investigations have also concluded that some bad characteristics of childhood get firmly rooted during adolescence. We should also note that some scientific researches have also revealed that changes occurring during adolescence are only natural. Hence one should not get unnecessarily worried on this score.

Adolescence Not Less Important than Childhood

Adolescence bridges the gulf between childhood and adulthood. This bridge is built on the basis of experiences acquired during childhood. If the beginning of any thing is not made during childhood, it is not possible to develop it during adolescence. That is why psychologists have stressed the need of proper and adequate education during childhood. It is not enough to consider adolescence as the bridge between only childhood and adulthood. Rather it may be considered as the base of adulthood on which rests the entire future of life. Attaching so much importance to adolescence does not minimise the importance of childhood. During adolescence the individual undergoes many kinds of changes including physical, mental, emotional, and social changes etc. If these changes are not properly channelized the individual will not become an ideal citizen, so adolescence should be given due importance.

Duration of Adolescence

According to psychologists adolescence starts at the age of 12 or 13 years. The dawn of adolescence is comparatively earlier in girls than in boys. Psychologists generally agree with the following developmental order of adolescence in boys and girls :

Boys :	Early Adolescence from 11 to 12½ or 13 years
	Middle Adolescence from 13 to 18 years
	Late Adolescence from 18 to 21 years
Girls :	Early adolescence from 10 to 11 years
	Middle Adolescence from 12 to 15 years
	Late Adolescence from 17 to 20 or 21 years.

Adolescence Important for All Types of Development

From the very start of adolescence sexual curiosities appear in boys and girls. From this time on, they start developing sexual maturity. In the process of attaining adulthood the individual's mental development also goes on along with his physical development. Physically the human being attains his or her maximum height and during adolescene the sexual organ, too, becomes well developed. Along with the mental development it is also expected that the individual's social and emotional outlooks also attain maturity. But the present-day society has become so complex that the individual's now requires some more time to achieve social and emotional maturity. As such, the adolescence is not enough. The emotional and social development, therefore, do not stop when the adolescence is over. However, adolescence is very important for all kinds of developments.

Feeling of Self-Consciousness during Adolescence

The individual is in a strange fix at the beginning of adolescence. At this stage he can neither be called a child nor an adult. During this period an adolescent faces many such problems about which he or she has to decide on one's own judgment. He develops a shy nature. The element of shyness is more intense in girls than in boys. This shyness is due to the development in body and certain tendencies in them. Although there is a rapid development of body during adolescence, but the individual is not able to exercise full control over the various parts of the body. Hence the individual is highly self-conscious at the dawn of adolescence. He generally tries to study the reactions of others towards his personality. After some time he is able to exercise control over his body. Then he feels less shy before others. He now, instead of running away from others, tries more in appearing before others.

An Order in the Development of Adolescence

There is an order in the development of adolescence as is found in the case of childhood. Although the development is of the same type, yet its speed differs from individual to individual. Some people think that certain developmental processes start suddenly, but scientific researches conclude otherwise. In fact, the developmental processes begin since infancy and gradually the individual appears as a changed man at the end of adolescence. There are many changes in his body and behaviour. He is now more mature physically, mentally, emotionally and socially. This change takes about seven or eight years. So it is difficult to mark changes every month or every year. During adolescence there is a kind of mental tension or conflict going on in the individual. This mental conflict, sometimes bursts out and others may notice it vividly. People sometimes think that adolescence is a stormy period in human life and the adolescent crosses the limits of acceptable social behaviour. In fact, there is nothing like this. Such things happen in the life of only those adolescents who have not been psychologically and sympathetically handled during childhood due to certain reasons, such as, loss of parents or unpsychological behaviour of elders. Unfavourable changes of environment or poverty may also be partially responsible for the adolescent rebelling against the standards set by the society.

PROBLEM OF ADJUSTMENT IN THE ENVIRONMENT

Some Problems before Adolescents

It has been indicated earlier that with the onset of adolescence there come many physical and mental changes in the individual. These two types of changes are accompanied by many other changes in the individual who feels all these changes but he fails to understand the causes of the same. He does not understand why his voice has become heavy and hoarse. He generally knows from others that his voice is not so sweet as before. The innocent and bright look of his face as during childhood is no more there. The friends of early childhood with whom he used to play do not appeal him now. He now develops a desire to know more about various body organs of the opposite sex. He develops a desire to observe them. He now shows keenness in reading those very books which he used to discard during his childhood. He shows now more liking for film shows. He also develops a desire to participate more in social activities. These new desires pose problems of adjustment in the new environment. If this problem of adjustment is not solved properly and psychologically, the adolescent is bound to develop inner conflicts. His mental peace is disturbed. The burden of solving these problems lies squarely on the shoulders of the adolescent. In the childhood the elderly people helped him without his asking for it. But now he does not receive that help because primarily he himself feels shy in putting his problems before them. Secondly, some of his problems are such that they are against the wishes of the parents. The adolescent also appears to defy the discipline which the guardian wants to impose on him. It is the tendency of the guardians to watch strictly the activities of the adolescents in order that they do not go out of their control. The guardians all the time try to snub the boy. The adolescent, on the other hand, thinks that he is getting mature and as such he should be treated like an adult. The adolescents who have received during their childhood training to stand on their own legs generally face less difficulty in facing these problems. In short, the adolescents have to face the following problems :

1. How to get rid of guardian's interference?
2. How to achieve some economic independence?
3. How to satisfy sexual desires?
4. How to spend the leisure time?
5. Which philosophy of life should be adopted?

Some Differences in the Problems of Adolescent Boys and Girls

Symonds has made a comparative study to find out the difference between various likings of adolescent boys and girls. He has found that their likings and problems are almost of the same type. Only there are differences in their degrees. Their most difficult problems relate to health, some economic independence, taste in studies and personal physical appearance. The problems of boys relate more to economic independence and informations connected with the opposite sex. The problems of girls relate mostly to efforts for making their appearance more attractive.

Needless to say that these problems make the problems of his adjustment in his environment more difficult.

Worries and Unhappiness in the Life of Adolescents

The adolescent feels worried due to the problem of adjustment. For example, one may point out to him that his voice has turned hoarse and rude. As a result, he begins to worry about it and tries to find out ways of making his voice as sweet as it used to be during his childhood. In comparison to social problems, the problems relating to his body become less important. The adolescent is now worried about his social behaviour. He tries to find out ways to adopt such behaviours which may enable him escape others' criticisms. Due to this worry it may be said that adolescents are full of worries and miseries. This worry also gives birth to undesirable aspects in their behaviours. We indicate here some of these undesirable elements in the character of the adolescent.

1. More carelessness in behaviour than before.
2. Less care of others' comforts.
3. Giving rude replies.
4. To become short-tempered and express displeasure.
5. Interfering in others' conversation.
6. Quarrelling with guardians for getting more freedom.
7. Beating the younger children in the home.
8. Appearing serious and engrossed in thinking.
9. Rejecting other people's advice and acting against it.
10. Showing no interest in ideals and principles.
11. Getting irritated on criticism by others.

The development of these things is quite natural. These things in the end prove helpful to him in his adjustment. Some guardians get nervous when they observe these things in the adolescent. They consider it as an insult hurled at them by the adolescents. Such attitude on the part of the guardians add insult to the injury of the adolescent and makes his life still more miserable.

It is psychologically a proper step on the part of guardians to send the adolescent to some other place when they find him worried in the effort to adjust in the environment. It may be helpful to lodge the adolescent in some good hostel for a year or two or send him to any relation or friend for some months. This will give him the desired freedom and some of his problems will be automatically solved. This will also enable him to achieve some degree of self-confidence and self-support. If the guardians do not help him in solving his problems, the adolescent may develop some defects in his personality and character. Evidently, guardians have an important role to play in solving the problems of the adolescent.

Adolescence : A Period of Transformation

We have already seen that adolescence is a stage of revolutionary changes in human life. The adolescent gives up old habits and acquires new outlooks. He has to shoulder new responsibilities. He has an additional worry of adjusting his personality in a new environment. At the end of adolescence he is able to establish his own personality, but before he is able to do so, there is a kind of instability in his behaviour. He is not firm in his views, principles and decisions. This instability is an indication of his immaturity. We generally find that an adolescent's behaviour is full of extremes. Either he will appear to be an extremely selfish person or extremely liberal. In the same way virtues and vices like smartness, lethargy, happiness or unhappiness, confidence or lack of confidence are also visible in him in a very high degree at some time or the other.

Desire to Learn New and Good Things during Adolescence

Fortunately this instability in the adolescent's behaviour does not prove to be a big hurdle in his adjustment, because he is all along trying to adjust himself. This effort soon makes him discard the element of instability in him. As a matter of fact, this nature of adolescence is necessary between childhood and adulthood, because it affords a good opportunity to the individual in order to get rid of old and bad habits. If the environment is psychological, the adolescent faces little difficulty in acquiring good habits.

Too Much Pampering during Childhood Create Difficulties during Adolescence

Those boys who have passed their childhood in an unpsychological atmosphere and have been too much pampered by their parents face many troubles during their adolescence. During adolescence the boy is expected to stand on his legs in many matters and shoulder responsibilities independently. If the boy has not been taught to be self-dependent during childhood, it becomes difficult for him to adopt that attitude during adolescence. He has to face many hardships in learning self-dependence. The result will be that his parents will interfere on every step and try that he carries out their wishes. They will never be able to teach him the lesson of self-dependence. This will have an adverse effect on the personality of the adolescent. He will continue to have a childish approach in many matters and will be afraid of facing the bitter truths of later life. It is, therefore, in the interest of the adolescent that the parents adopt a psychological approach towards their children.

ADOLESCENCE : A PERIOD OF PROBLEMS

Adolescents' Own Problems

Each stage of development in human life has its own problems. The problems of childhood are no less important. The parents and the teachers are always worried about them. What we have discussed so far also indicates that adolescent, too, face strange problems. But the difference between the problems of childhood and those of adolescence is that whereas the child remains practically unconcerned and unworried about most of his problems, the adolescent himself is deeply worried about the same. Child's problems are mostly the problems of parents while adolescent's problems are mostly his own problems and he cannot shift the responsibility of solving them to his parents or teachers. Not only this, the neighbours and the society, too, sometimes are worried about the problems of an adolescent. For example, if an adolescent becomes immoral, corrupt, he poses a danger to the society.

Problems of Adolescents are Natural

The problems of adolescents appear to us complex, because we judge and compare them with the normal behaviour of an adult. We do so perhaps because in physical appearance the adolescent appears more like an adult and not like a child. Moreover, we have as yet not determined a definite standard to judge the conduct of adolescents. However, we have to note that adolescence is not a problem period but a stage in the human development which has certain strange but natural problems.

Difficulties in the Study of Adolescence

Psychologists are faced with many difficulties in the study of adolescent behaviour. For the study of problems relating to adolescents good material is available only in educational institutions because a fairly good number of adolescents of different types are found there. Unfortunately managers and other officials of educational institutions do not extend the necessary cooperation. They do not consider such studies important and useful. They think that conducting of such a study will affect the daily routine of the school. They further think that during investigation if a questionnaire contains questions relating to religion, sex, friends and family relations, the boys may come to know certain undesirable things which will not have beneficial effect on their character. The parents and guardians, too, do not evince a cooperative attitude towards this.

Non-Cooperation of Adolescents

What to say of parents and the school, even the adolescents themselves are not interested in such a study. They think that the questions in the questionnaire interfere in their private life. They, therefore, sometimes intentionally supply wrong answers to the questions contained in the questionnaire. Much knowledge may be gained on the basis of the observation of the behaviour of children, but this cannot be said about adolescent's behaviour, because they do not allow others to peep into their doings.

Supply of Wrong Information by the Parents

Some parents and guardians may be approached to supply informations when reliable informations are not obtained from schools, colleges and adolescents. But the informations supplied by them, too, are often exaggerated. Some parents say that their son or daughter does not indulge in this or that activity, although the fact may be otherwise.

Adolescents in Colleges and Schools Not the True Representatives of Common Adolescents

As the child grows, the individual differences in his character also develop. There is a greater similarity in the character of young children, while it is not so in the case of adolescents. Besides heredity, the social and economic status are also responsible for many differences in their behaviour. The curriculum should also be based in accordance with such variations in the behaviour. Only then by scrutinising their all-round development reliable information may be obtained about them. In the absence of proper education many adolescents give up their studies, because they do not find the education beneficial. Hence it is difficult to find all types of adolescent in schools and colleges. In such circumstances, researches carried out on adolescents in colleges and schools do not give a true picture of common adolescents.

Lack of Necessary Resources

Psychologists have not yet succeeded in producing proper resources for the study of behaviour of adolescents. The resources and methods applied in case of children do not yield valid results when applied to adolescents.

METHODS OF ADOLESCENT'S STUDY

Many methods are applied in the study of adolescents' behaviour, but no single method has given satisfactory results. So various methods are applied to obtain various kinds of informations.

Observation Method

This method is not helpful because adolescents try to keep their activities secret. When they learn that someone is studying their behaviour, they give up that particular behaviour for the time being.

Questionnaire Method

Personal interview may yield better results because then the psychologist may know as to which of the answers are being correctly answered and which ones wrongly. But when the adolescents are asked to give written replies they often supply wrong informations.

Retrospective Report

Sometimes this method yields very good results and valuable informations are obtained. In this method adults are asked questions relating to any particular stage of adolescence. Mature persons or adults have comparatively a better understanding and they do not hesitate in giving correct informations. But sometimes they also give wrong information because it is not unnatural that they may forget some facts due to lapse of time. The other shortcoming in this method is that due to a change in social and economic status their reaction to a particular stage of adolescence may be influenced because of their mature experiences. So it is not very reliable to base one's findings on the information given by adults about their adolescence.

Psycho-analytic Method

This method is not very helpful. It is possible through this method to study some problems of only some adolescents, but its application on common adolescent does not yield trustworthy results. This method only throws light on problem of adolescents.

Adolescent Diary

Through the study of adolescents' diaries valuable and important information may be gathered, because the adolescents express their views freely in their diaries. They do so because they have no fears that others will read them. Their memory is also fresh while writing the diary. But the difficulty in this method is that only very few, if any, keep diaries. Hence such diaries are not available in large number. It is, therefore, not good to reach a conclusion on the basis of a few diaries. Another shortcoming of this method is that the adolescent while writing the diary is under emotional strain and he may exaggerate the facts.

Facts Disclosed by Teachers, Doctors and Sports-Organisers

They have some importance in the study of adolescents. The experiences of teachers, doctors and sports-organisers throw some light on the behaviour of adolescents. First of all there is no place for exaggeration in the observation of this class of people. Secondly, their conclusion is based on many experiences. But their observations are likely to be somewhat one-sided, because the adolescents are very careful in their behaviour towards these persons.

Genetic Case Study or Developmental Method

In this method a single individual's different stages of development are studied. This method is applied in different environments on several girls and boys for some years for achieving reliable results. In this way the changes occurring at a particular age are easily studied. But it is not easy to find an adolescent at one place for several years. This difficulty is encountered in this method. The other hurdle in the application of this method is that to study different aspects of a developmental stage is itself not an easy task. So it becomes desirable to limit the scope of study. For example, it is more convenient to limit the scope to either 'social development', 'changes in personality' or 'likings in studies' etc. This limited field of study may give more reliable and satisfactory results. Similarly, if each investigator chooses one of the different aspects of adolescence development, it will then be possible to gather more reliable informations.

SUMMARY

Adolescence is a stage in human life. During this period the body undergoes revolutionary changes. The mind and its outlook, too, experience important changes. The adolescent at the end of this period resembles the adult and leaves childhood far behind. The changes include physical, mental, social and emotional.

Adolescence starts at the age of 12 or 13 years. In girls it appears earlier. In girls this stage starts at the age of 11 years or so and lasts till 17 or 19 years. In boys the period begins at the age of 12½ or 13 years and goes upto the age of 20 or 21 years of age.

The adolescent is a period of worry and anxieties for the boy because with rapid physical and mental changes he has to face the problem of adjustment in the new environment. He appears worried, miserable, stormy, intolerant and a rebel. The main problems before the adolescent are to acquire some economic independence, get rid of parental interferences, fulfilment of desires, how to spend leisure and which philosophy of life he should adopt. There is some difference between the problems of boys and girls. They develop some undesirable traits. These are generally negligence, discourtesy, short-temper, interference in other people's business, intoleration, beating young children etc.

The parents have a responsibility towards the adolescent and they have to deal with him psychologically and sympathetically.

These are many difficulties in the study of adolescence. Some of these are lack of cooperation from guardians and teachers of schools and colleges, non-cooperation of the adult himself, wrong information tendered by the parents and lack of resources.

Seven methods are used in the study of adolescent. These are : (1) Observation Method, (2) Questionnaire Method, (3) Personal Interview, (4) Retrospective Method, (5) Psycho-analytic Method, (6) Adolescent's diary, and (7) Genetic Case Studies or Developmental Method.

Exercises

1. What are the Chief Characteristics of adolescence?
2. 'Adolescence is a period of stress and strain'. Comment.
3. Explain how adolescence is not less important than childhood ?
4. What are the problems that an adolescent generally confronts ?
5. Distinguish between the problems of an adolescent boy and those of an adolescent girl.
6. How should we deal with our adolescents in view of their various difficulties and problems?

2

Puberty

Definition

Puberty may be defined as that period in human life when the bodily and genital organs of an individual start developing very fast and in that process they reach their full development. Puberty is not an independent period of development. It may at best be called a part of adolescence. Adolescence includes an individual's physical, mental, social, emotional, moral, spiritual and all other developments. But puberty is mostly concerned with bodily development. In fact, puberty is the beginning of adolescence. We will discuss its salient features below.

Procreation Power Makes its Appearance in an Individual with the Start of Adolescence

We have already mentioned that by the time adolescence starts, the boys and girls develop the natural power of procreation. People believe that with the start of menstruation in the girl she becomes capable of conceiving. When the parents in India come to know that their daughter's menstruation has started they generally begin to think that they should get her married soon. Perhaps the belief that the girl has become capable of conception is the main cause for this thinking and worry. As far as boys are concerned, it is somewhat difficult to determine the period when they develop the reproductive capacity, but it is thought that when nocturnal emissions start the boy develops the power to procreate. However, scientist hold the view that it is not always correct to assume this. Of course, this may be regarded as a sign of puberty's start. But the procreation power takes some time to mature.

Difficult to Determine Correct Time of Maturity—Boys Behind Girls

Bodily changes begin in boys and girls with the setting in the early adolescence, but the power to procreate is not fully realised. During the middle of adolescence, this power of procreation comes up but bodily changes still continue. During this stage all powers relating to procreation almost reach maturity and genital organs of boys and girls get fully developed. It is difficult to tell the age at which the sexual maturation is reached. Different adolescents reach this stage of maturity at different ages. But this is generally accepted that normally girls at the age of 13½ years and boys at the age of 14½ years enter the middle of adolescence. The changes in the body of girls and boys at the age of 14 years are clearly visible. According to studies conducted by psychologists more than 50 per cent of girls' menstruation starts between the age of 12½ to 14½ years. As far as boys are concerned 50 per cent or more reach middle of adolescence between 14 to 15½ years of age. Shuttle Worth's studies reveal that in attaining maturity boys are behind the girls by a year or two.

Heredity and Environment Influence Age of Sexual Maturation

Variations in the age of individuals as regards sexual maturation is influenced by several factors. Heredity or family traditions may also influence it. Food, climate, diseases etc. which are related to environment also affect the sexual maturation age. It has been generally observed that girls belonging to countries which have a warm climate, and also those who lead a luxurious life reach sexual maturation earlier as compared to those living in cold climate or those who do hard labour to earn their bread. In India, which has a warm climate, girls mature sexually early.

Inter-Relation between Mental Development and Sexual Maturity

Mental development appears to be linked with sexual maturation, but in the absence of sufficient proofs it is difficult to prove it. Some researches conducted in Western countries prove that menstruation starts early in girls who have a sharp intellect than those girls who are dull. Similarly, intellectually superior boys also reach sexual maturation earlier than dull boys. According to the findings of Lutz the process of sexual maturation starts at the age of 12½ years in intellectually superior boys, at the age of 13½ years in normal boys and at the age of 14½ years in dull boys. Hollingworth has also reached the conclusion that menstruation starts early in intellectually superior girls. Terman has also tried to prove this theory.

Sexual Maturation in Boys takes a Longer Period

Some more time is required for sexual maturation in boys when they reach the stage of middle adolescence. The scientists have studied this subject very thoroughly. They agree that boys take a longer period for sexual maturation as compared to girls. There is, of course, some individual variations in time. Some boys attain sexual maturation in three years while some others take five years. It may be said safely that girls attain sexual maturation in three to three and a half years, while boys take two to four years. This means that there is more uniformity in girls. Girls in whom the process of sexual maturation starts late, attain sexual maturation early and those in whom the process starts early the sexual maturation takes a longer period. The period of childhood is short for those who attain sexual maturation early and such persons do not enjoy for a longer period the liberties of childhood. They, however, enjoy a longer period of adolescence and this enables them a better opportunity for proper social and emotional adjustment.

Changes relating to Sexual Organs in Boys

This has already been said earlier that the male organ starts increasing in size with the advent of adolescence. The male organ is very small during childhood, but with the coming of adolescence it increases in length and girth. Gradually pubic hairs appear around the root of the male organ. Some persons regard it as a sign of sexual maturity. The male organ gets erect at the time of sexual intercourse. Even sexual desire makes the organ erect. Erection is also natural when the individual feels great pressure in the urinary bladder. Some adolescents get scared when nocturnal emission takes place. The guardians are also to be blamed for it, because they inject wrong theories in the adolescent's mind. The friends also tell him wrong things about it because they themselves are ignorant of facts. Generally common people think that nocturnal emission is a sign of lack of potency or is a sign of some disease. Nocturnal emission is a perfectly normal process. The modern scientists adhere to this theory. There can be a number of causes leading to nocturnal emissions commonly known as night dreams. Sometimes entertaining sexual desire causes it. It is caused also by eating too much food, checking the pressure of urination, sleeping in a wrong posture, wearing tight clothes, constipation or sleeping on a luxurious bed etc. Some adolescents frequently get night dreams and some rarely. Scientists hold the view that the body itself ejects out semen which is in excess. It is simply a folly to worry on account of night dreams and it is absolutely necessary to acquaint the adolescent with adequate knowledge about the subject.

Other Changes

In our country the voice of a boy undergoes a change at the age of 13½ or 14 years. The voice turns heavy, deep and slightly rough. Its earlier sweetness disappears but the adolescent realises it at the age on 16 or 17 years.

Generally, pubic hairs make their appearance near about the age of 14 years. By the end of the fifteenth year the hairs clearly grow out. Then hairs start appearing in the arm-pit and later on it starts appearing over the face. In the beginning the hair is brown in colour and thinly spread. Gradually, its number as well as darkness increases. In some the growth of hair is so fast that he has to start shaving them as early as 16 or 17 years. In many the growth is so little and they even do not need shaving at the age of 20 years. By the end of middle adolescence pimples appear on the faces of some adolescents. At the end of adolescence stage, a person develops his shoulders, chest, arms and legs. These limbs are fully developed and the adolescent appears more like an adult.

Changes in Reproductory Organs of Girls

Most of the parts of the reproductory organ lies inside the body of the girl. They start developing gradually during adolescence. The belly of the girl increases due to this development. She sometimes feels much embarrassed before friends due to the abdominal growth. We have mentioned earlier that with the start of menstruation the girl is considered to be more mature than earlier. In fact, she is now considered a woman. If the menstruation takes place after 28 days regularly it is regarded as a sign of good health. In India if menstruration starts at the age of 13 or 13½ years, it is considered normal and natural. Sometimes it starts a bit late or becomes irregular. It stops generally between the age of 45 to 50 years. With the onset of menopause the woman loses her power to conceive. Although the cycle of 28 days is considered natural, yet there are occasions when it becomes irregular. If health is not good, the menstruation stops for many months after its first appearance. Normally bleeding continues for four days during menstruation but sometimes it stops after one day or may also continue from 6 to 10 days. During the menstruation period the experiencing of pain in the belly, irritation in vagina or other troubles relating to reproductory organs are natural. In such situation it is advisable to consult a physician.

Development of Breasts : Growth of Hairs

The first external sign in the girl of sexual maturity is the development of breasts. It takes three years for the breast to get fully developed and reach their normal size. During this period the hips too develop sufficiently. Their girth also increases and becomes round in shape. Hairs also make their appearance around the vagina. Then hairs grow in the arm-pit also. Sometimes it is seen that hairs appear before menstruation and sometimes it appears after menstruation. The development of breasts and hips and the appearance of hairs are the definite signs of onset of sexual maturity.

Voice Sweeter : Body Gains Weight

During adolescence the voice of a girl becomes sweeter and tone gets slow. Now her shoulders widen and with the gaining of weight her limbs get into shape. In the beginning all these changes are more visible in boys.

Psychological Importance of Physical Changes during Adolescence

All the changes happening in the body during adolescence in boys and girls have far reaching psychological importance. The speed of physical changes influence the degree of psychological effect. Prior preparation is necessary to give right direction to adolescents when they enter this stage. Even in this modern and scientific age some uncivilised tribes give particular attention to this aspect of life and the adolescents have to remain under control and training for a certain period. During this period the girls and the boys have to remain away from their families. It is really surprising to note that we the so-called civilised people do not pay attention towards this kind of training and education. We have taken it for granted that the adolescent has to solve his problems himself and when he fails to solve his problems we indiscriminately criticise and condemn him. This makes the life of an adolescent difficult and miserable. The adolescent boy out of sheer shyness remains perturbed while the girls when their delicate feelings get hurt out of helpness weep. It is, therefore, necessary for the parents to approach in a psychological manner towards adolescents' problems and arrange proper training and education of the boys and girls in this sphere.

EFFECT OF DEVELOPMENT OF SEXUAL ORGANS

The boy gets perturbed on seeing his sexual organ developing rapidly. He always tries to ensure that it does not come to the notice of others. Sometimes, he does not know what to do when his sexual organ gets erected without his desiring so. This is because he does not know why this happens. Nocturnal emissions leave spots on his clothes. This places him in an embarrassing situation. He also feels pleasure in handling his sexual organ. So he develops the habit of masturbation. In the early stage he is too much inclined and practises masturbation frequently, but later on he develops social fear and does not gather courage to come face to face with others.

Girls Feel Shy when Menstruation takes place for the First Time

The girl is less conscious towards development in her reproductory organs because much of the development is internal, but she gets worried when menstruation starts. She feels perturbed about what others might be thinking about her. She feels shy in appearing before her elders in the home.

Shyness and Worry in Girls when Bosom and Hips Develop

Shyness and worry in girls increase considerably when her breasts and hips develop. She thinks that others must be observing these developments even when she was wearing clothes. This creates a feeling of shyness in the girl. She, therefore, tries to wear such garments which help her hide this development in the body. She also tries to walk with bowed shoulders. This adversely affect the beauty of the girl. She also tries to hide the development of hips and tries to reduce their size by reducing her diet.

General Development and its Effect on Mental Outlook

By the time the adolescence is over the boys and girls think that they have become adults. So they think that they should also get the rights and privileges enjoyed by adults. They do not relish the control of parents or guardians. They want to exercise their free will or freedom in their activities. They do not like that elders should interfere or give directions in matters relating to dress, books or visits to other places.

Effect of the General Built of Body and its Stature

The adolescent by listening to the remarks of other people generally come to know what constitutes a good or an ugly physique. If the personality of an adolescent boy does not radiate manliness, and if others criticise, he feels ashamed. Similarly, girls also develop a sense of inferiority if their body does not reflect feminine looks and touches. These complexes leave unhealthy effect and there is always a fear about their developing a sense of inferiority complex. H.R. Stoltz and L.M. Stoltz studied 92 boys. Of these 21 were worried about their physical beauty, 8 felt perturbed due to pimples and scars on their faces, one did not like the quality of his skin, four were dissatisfied about the development of their chests and two were worried about the size of their sexual organ. Some adolescents do not like the shape of their shoulders and therefore remain worried. Some dislike the fat around their waste and some others feel that the size of their sexual organ is small. The cause of this fear, shyness, worry or satisfaction is the standards set up by the adults. The adolescents judge their body and organs against these standards and either feel satisfied or dissatisfied.

Adolescent Girls comparatively More Worried about their Appearances

Like boys, the girls too judge their physical developments against the standards set by the society. If she does not fare better against these standards, she feels worried. She feels greatly ashamed if she is too tall or short, too thick or thin or dark skinned, because she has to face taunts from others. She also dislikes too big or too short hands or abnormal size of legs. Too much hairs on the body or appearance of hairs on face also cause worry in her.

It is generally observed that as compared to boys, girls are more conscious about their physical appearance. This does not mean that boys are indifferent in this respect. However, the girls are comparatively more anxious to hide their ugliness. Psychologists of European and American countries say that in order to give a raised appearance to their breasts girls use padded brassiers. They put on high-heeled shoes in order to give a smaller appearance to their feet. And if they are generously proportioned they start dieting to get slimmer.

Change of Voice — Boys comparatively More Concerned

Both boys and girls become somewhat shy with the change of voice. So they do not relish speaking or singing before others. The unpsychological approach of parents, guardians and friends is responsible for this element of shyness and hesitation among the adolescents. If these persons refrain from unpsychological utterances the life of the adolescent will not then be so much miserable. It is a matter of great regret that these very persons forget the days of their own adolescence. In the matter of change in voice boys comparatively get more embarrassed, because the girl's voice does not undergo so much change. It remains comparatively sweeter than that of boys.

Moustache and Beard Embarrass Boys

The boy gets somewhat worried when moustache and beard grow on his face. Earlier, he does not realise that at this age every boy gets them. He wants to hide them through shaving. He also feels embarrassed at the appearance of too many hair on the body.

Girls Extremely worried from Moustache and Beard

If the girls get any indication of appearance of moustache and beard on her face she is greatly worried. She desperately tries to remove them. She does not hesitate to buy anything that can root them out permanently.

Abnormal size of Hands, Legs and Nose cause worry in the Girl

As compared to other limbs, hands, legs and nose reach their full development earlier. Their abnormally big size goes against the recognised standard of feminine beauty. So the girl gets worried if these organs of her body are too big. She can hide her big feet by wearing high-heeled shoes, but how can she hide the abnormal length of her hands or nose whenever she sees the reflection of her nose in water or mirror she is pained. She is, therefore, unable to get rid of this type of mental torture.

First Menstruation worries Girls

The girl is very much disturbed when the menstruation begins for the first time in her life. Her first feeling is that she has got some wound somewhere inside her body. This feeling gives her mental worry which sometimes increases her physical trouble during menstruation. The parents want to keep knowledge about menstruation a secret with the result that although knowing it fully well that each girl experiences menstruation or menstruation is a natural process with every woman, the girl develops hatred and fear for it. This sometimes so adversely affects her that fear and hatred towards menstruation take firm root in her mind on a permanent basis. Later in their lives, if during menstruation they do not experience any bodily trouble, they get worried. It is also the experience of many mature women.

During adolescence the girl is instilled with the feeling that menstruation is a dirty physical process and it is impossible to get rid of it till the age of 45 or 50 years. She is told not to discuss it with anyone except the parents, the doctor or an intimate girl friend. In this manner the girl has to bear an emotional shock in respect of menstruation. She, therefore, considers it a permanent curse. If during menstruation she feels pain in body her feeling towards it become all the more torturing. She considers boys more lucky because they are free from this process. So it is not surprising that she turns unsocial and short-tempered during this period.

Difficult to Study Psychological Importance of Menstruation

So far much attention has not been paid for any special study of the psychological study of menstruation. It is almost impossible to get correct answers from adolescent girls because due to their natural shyness they will not correctly reply to queries. Secondly, many schools and colleges will neither permit nor provide facilities for this type of study. Some mature women have, of course, been studied in this respect. This study has revealed that during menstruation women feel lethargy and fatigue. They also become somewhat gloomy, so women do not like to do any work during menstruation. The reactions of adolescent girls towards their first menstruation is influenced by the general knowledge they possess about menstruation at that time. If her mother or friend had explained to her in a psychological manner the significance of menstruation, then her worry is lessened. E.S. Conklin[1] studied the reaction of 475 adolescent girls towards their first menstruation. Fifty-one per cent of them said that they remained indifferent towards it, 24 per cent expressed their anxiety, 12 per cent felt a shock to their sense of pride, seven per cent had fear, while six per cent were happy.

Feeling of Sexual Desire on Achieving Maturity

The girls mature earlier than the boys. On maturing, their taste differs from those of boys. Girls in middle adolescence develop desire to know things related to sex. They also get curious to know about boys' sexual development and activities. They will not hesitate to establish close relations with boys, if there is no social restrictions. Those girls in whom menstruation has not yet started or those who are in the early adolescence stage remain indifferent towards these sexual activities and desires.

Psychological Importance of Early or Late Maturity

The psychological importance of early or late maturation is no less important. Those girls who reach early maturation do not like the company of girls of their age group who have not yet reached maturation, because they start feeling having a higher status in the society. They also do not like to mix with younger girls. But the trouble is that it is not easy for them to adjust themselves with those who are senior to them because in that case they have not reached that standard of culture, behaviour and knowledge which the elder girls and women have reached. These very facts apply equally in the case of boys. Those who attain late sexual maturity also have to face similar reactions. Sometimes those adolescents who attain late maturity behave in such a manner as if they have become adults. They become ridiculous because it does not look decent on their part to copy the behaviour of mature persons.

Effect of Beginning of Adolescence on Behaviour

With the start of adolescence far reaching changes take place in the nature and behaviour of the adolescent. Sometimes, this behaviour undergoes so much change that parents and guardians are taken aback. Fortunately, greater part of this behaviour is distasteful. Many of the behaviours of adolescents appear unsocial and unsympathetic. It appears whatever good things the boys had learnt during childhood, they are forgetting now and are treading on wrong path. Buhler has, therefore, defined this period as a negative phase. A great change in the behaviour of adolescent is witnessed between 6 to 32 months after the start of adolescence. Buhler studies the diaries of adolescents and came to know that six to twelve months before the start of adolescence the boys experience a great mental unrest. It does not want to keep himself fettered by any social value. According to Buhler the boys resent and express displeasure in carrying out orders given by others. They show lack of interest, impertinence, anger, lethargy, indifference towards the work given to them by others. They also hate themselves and entertain a kind of contempt for the society. This reaction is visible both in girls and boys. Hetzer, in his study has supported the conclusions of Buhler. Vecerka conducted his studies on 1492 girls and reached the conclusion that girls generally like to remain aloof and dislike work before the start of adolescence.

Feeling of Dissatisfaction

The girls develop a feeling of dissatisfaction when the adolescence phase of life starts. People think that this dissatisfaction is unreasonable. A glimpse of this dissatisfaction may be had from their general behaviour. An adolescent boy often disobeys elders. He feels that other forcibly want to keep him under control. As such, he sometimes rebels. He finds fault with every one in the house.

Conduct of the Adolescent

An adolescent seldom has respect for others. A kind of indifference may be noticed in many of his behaviours. He has no definite ideal. So there is no stability in his behaviour towards any ideal. The influence of environment is unavoidable. So it affects his behaviour. Therefore, there is less dissatisfaction in an adolescent of the family where a healthy environment pervades. In the early phase of adolescence the adolescent tries to find fault with the behaviour of other boys in his age group. He does not want to leave any such opportunity. He, therefore, limits the circle of his friends. He does not like to associate himself with a group. So he retains only one or two friends. It is true that during the middle phase of adolescence boys and girls are attracted towards each other, but this is not so in the early phase. In the early phase of adolescence they are indifferent towards each other.

Emotion Dominates

Boys and girls are very emotional in the beginning of adolescence. Their emotions are, therefore, easily hurt. An eleven years old girl gets emotional easily and begins to weep or expresses anger by sitting in the corner of the house. Similarly, a twelve years boy is also extremely emotional and does not lag behind the girl in this respect. But one has to concede that girls under the pressure of emotion resort to weeping more than boys do, because it is not possible for them to rebel like boys or adopt a defiant attitude like them. Therefore, the greatest weapon in their armoury at this phase of life is weeping.

Making Castles in the Air

During adolescence the individual often thinks that he is loved by none. The adolescent defies elders and does not like the company of many persons. Therefore, he develops the habit of making castles in air. He chalks out ambitious plans for his future life. In making these imaginary schemes he enjoys both pleasure and pain. But most of the psychologists are of the opinion that in this kind of act the adolescent suffers more pain than pleasure.

Curiosity to Gain Knowledge regarding the Development of Sexual Organ

When observing the development of sexual organs the adolescent naturally thinks of others. He becomes curious to know about the similar changes taking place in others of his age group. He is curious to know the reasons for this development. The girls and boys are extremely curious to know each other's sexual developments. They have heard in the past many things about the various changes that take place during adolescence. But their curiosities remain unsaid in the absence of personal experiences. After getting personal experiences the boys and girls like to relate and confirm their experiences with other friends.

Improved Behaviour by Later Adolescence

The adolescent reaches a curious stage of his development by the end of middle phase of adolescence. At this stage his behaviours may be so distasteful and troublesome for others that this phase may be called the 'Problematic Period'. But at the end of middle adolescence phase there is a sudden improvement in the adolescent's behaviour. He now appears comparatively more social, smart and active. He is more sympathetic towards others. He is not so much worried and dissatisfied now. He is also not much inclined to find fault with others. There is an all-round improvement in his behaviour and he further strives to improve his behaviour.

SUMMARY

The puberty is that phase of life which serves as a link between childhood and adulthood. The child during this period is transformed into an adult. The most important development during this phase is the physical development. The individual attains his maximum height and his sexual organs get fully developed. He becomes capable of procreation. This development is of course influenced by the environment and heredity. There also appears some relation between the mental development and the sexual development, though it is difficult to prove it.

During this phase besides the development of male organ and the reproductory organs in girls pubic hairs make their appearance around the genital organs and arm pits. The voice changes. This change in voice is more prominent in boys. In the girls there hips and breasts develop.

The period of adolescence is a period of mental agony for both boys and girls. They feel restless, do not like to take interest in work, feel shy in appearing before elders, entertain fear, doubts and frustration. They are also very emotional in their approach. The girls under emotional impact frequently weep; the boys adopt defiant attitude and rebel against elders. They want more economic and other independence. They resent elders control and do not observe discipline. They also try to live aloof. The girls are particularly worried about their physical appearance and try to appear more beautiful.

Another important development during this phase of life in girls is the start of menstruation. Due to ignorance, unpsychological understanding of parents and lack of proper education it is very troublesome period in a girl's life. She is bewildered and does not know what to do on the first appearance of menstruation.

At the end of adolescence the boys and girls behaviour improves considerably. They turn social and sympathetic towards others, because by that time they succeed in adjusting themselves. It is the duty of parents to approach the adolescent's problems psychologically and educate him properly in this respect. This would save the adolescent from many worries and help in his proper and timely adjustment.

Exercises

1. Describe the special characteristics on the onset of puberty.
2. Describe the main changes that occur in boys and girls during puberty.
3. What are the effects of various physical changes on the outlook of adolescents?
4. What should the parents do for a healthier growth of adolescents?

NOTE

1. E.S. Conklin, *Principle of Adolescent Psychology*, Holt, New York, 1933.

3

Significance of Physical Changes

Earlier it was not considered necessary to study the physical development of adolescents, because the psychologists and others were not sure of its impact on the mental, social and emotional development. Gradually, the researchers of psychologists have convinced the people that the physical development in adolescence largely contributes to the development of the personality of an individual. We shall see now how it contributes to the development of individual's personality.

Relationship between Physical and other Developments

The physical development greatly influences the general development of the adolescent. His emotional, social and mental developments are very much related to physical development. If the physical development does not proceed properly the adolescent may develop inferiority and other complexes and his emotional development will suffer and he may become short-tempered. Consequently, social development on correct lines will not be possible. He will then join the company of bad persons. Thus the physical development of an adolescent is closely related to other developments. Here we shall refer to only those physical and physiological developments which affect the behaviour of adolescents.

METHODS OF STUDIES OF PHYSICAL DEVELOPMENT

Retest and Sampling Methods

Two methods of studies of physical development are generally prevalent. The first method is known as 'Retest'. According to this method different limbs and organs of the adolescent are measured each year and then results are compared to assess the rate of normal and abnormal growth. The other method is known as the 'Sampling' method in which different adolescents belonging to different age groups are compared and attempts are made to assess the rate of normal and abnormal development of a particular adolescent. Although in the case of the first method much statistics are not available, yet it is more reliable because it gives full information about an adolescent's development. The second method only gives a general idea of physical development. In this method the comparative study involves at least 10,000 adolescents, otherwise the results will not be reliable.

EXTERNAL PHYSICAL CHANGES

Fast Speed of Development in Early Adolescence

Adolescence is that phase in human life when the speed of development is at the top. It may be compared with the speed of growth from the time he is conceived till he is of six months in age. The speed of development remain high till the age of six years and then it slows down, but with the coming of early adolescence, the speed of development again goes up. This speed continues for a year or two and then again it slows down as in the past. At the time of birth the boy is 1/3 inch taller than the girl. At the age of five years this difference increases to 1/2 inch. At the age of 11 years both are of the same height. At the age of 13 years the girl is 3/4 inch taller than the boy. They are again equal in height at the age of 15 years and the boy shows a tendency to go ahead. At the age of 18 years the boy is 2½ to 3 inches taller than the girl.

Individual Differences in Development

With the physical development the behaviour of adolescents also undergoes a change. We find individual differences in this development. For example, a girl or a boy may differ in physical development when compared with other boys and girls of the same age group. Some adolescents develop early physically while some others take a longer time for their full physical development. It is not necessary that all physical organs may follow a definite pattern of development in case of late physical development. Consequently, some limbs develop early and some late. Viewed from the point of view of physical development, the early development may be useful for the adult but viewed from a social angle it proves only harmful. By early development the individual does not feel happy in the company of those who belong to his own age group, because to him they appear younger. In the society of elders he feels difficulty in mental adjustment since elders appear mentally more mature. In this way socially he feels aloof.

Height

It is to be noted that height and weight do not depend on age, but depend on the advent of adolescence. The development in height, weight and strength generally come simultaneously. All these develop considerably during early or pre-adolescence. Individual differences in relation to height may be seen easily in all age groups. This difference is not so much visible during childhood as in early or middle adolescence. Van Dyke[1] observed that girls develop considerably in height during pre-adolescence period. He has concluded that on an average for some time they gained 2.9 inches every year. The girls attain much height between 10 to 14 years and boys between 12 to 16 years. By the end of adolescence the individual gains his full height.

Weight

With the development of bones and muscles the weight of adolescent increases. In children it is the fat which gives them weight because their bones and muscles have not yet developed. During the pre-adolescence phase the bones and muscles start increasing and fat decreases so during this time the boys and girls appear lean and thin, although their weight increases. This increase in weight is due to the development of muscles, bones and increase in height. During childhood boys weigh more than girls, but during the period of 10 to 15 years girls generally weigh more than boys. After 15 years again the boys weigh more than the girls.

Head and Face

Scientists are of the opinion that at the age of three years the size of child's head is 86 per cent of that of an adult. At the age of six it comes to 90 per cent. It is only 5 or 6 per cent less than that of an adult at the age of 14 years. The change in face is slight during childhood, but during adolescence it changes to a large extent. During this period the growth is mostly in length. There is a slight change in the breadth. The mouth becomes slightly broad and lips become more beautiful. The upper part of the mouth develops early. The nose also become a bit long and wide. The face becomes slightly broad and lips becomes thicker. The full development of jaws comes last. The angle of the jaws also changes during the process of development. This effects great change in the face.

Trunk

The development of chest takes place at a rapid pace between the age of 14 to 16 or 17 years. At the end of the adolescence the length of the trunk increases three times as that during of childhood. During adolescence the waist is quite visible. It is distinct, now. The hips of girls start developing rapidly from the age of 12 years. The boys are a year or two behind the girls in this process of development.

Legs and Arms

At the time of birth the legs are one-third of the total height. At maturity legs are about one half of the total height. The bones of legs are very small during childhood. During adolescence these bones increase four times and are generally longer than the trunk. The legs of those who mature early are shorter than the trunk. In those who mature late the legs are generally bigger than the trunk. In short-statured people the legs as compared to trunk are generally smaller. In between the age of 10 to 14 years the thighs and calfs develop rapidly. Their girth increases rapidly. The arms also increase considerably during adolescence. In the beginning they appear to be longer than other limbs of the body. The arms are slightly short of those persons who attain early maturity.

Bones

We have already observed earlier that during adolescence there is a tremendous development in bones. The adolescent's height increases by two inches from mere development of leg bones. With the increase in backbone the trunk of the adolescent increases in length. The face also develops in size due to the development of bones. The lower jaw now appears big and powerful. Consequently, the chin also appears enlarged. The bones not only change in appearance but the matter in it also changes. During the childhood the bones are weak and soft. With the change of matter inside them they become harder and stronger. The skeleton in the body of girls gets fully developed at the age of 17 years. The boys take two more years. Their skeleton gets fully developed when they are 19 years old. The development of skeleton is deeply related to the development of genital organs. Generally, they mature simultaneously. At the end of adolescence all the teeth spring out in the mouth.

Muscles

The development of muscles is necessary with the development of bones. Therefore, muscles also grow rapidly during adolescence. With the development of muscles the body becomes heavier and more handsome. At the age of 8 years muscles weigh 27 per cent of total body weight, at 15 it is 32 per cent and at 16 years of age the percentage is 44. When muscles outgrow in proportion to bones the body looks ugly. Contrary to this if muscles do not grow in proportion to bones the body appears lean and thin and the individual gives the appearance of a sick man. The girls in comparison to boys put less manual labour. Consequently, their muscles develop less in comparison to boys who have to do more physical labour.

Environment for the use of Developed Power

With the development of muscles the strength of the body also increases. But the development of muscles alone is not sufficient for the increase of strength. It needs proper freedom, discipline, education and good environment. During adolescence the strength of body increases tremendously. It is necessary to utilise this energy properly or else the life of the adolescent will become lethargic and miserable. The children use their energy by running here and there often aimlessly, but it is not possible in the case of the adolescent to run here and there aimlessly in order to consume the energy. His physical labour must have an object to achieve, otherwise he will not do physical labour. He finds some purpose in the game of hockey or football and therefore he plays them willingly. However, if there is no aim before the adolescent, his energy will get misdirected. If this state of affairs continues for a long time, the adolescent will lose interest in life.

Lack of Balance in Adolescents

There is a great change in the balance of ordinary actions with the development of muscles. As a result, there is a loss of balance in manual work. There are occasions when the adolescent loses balance during physical work, for instance falling down of an article carried in the hands, getting disbalanced while walking or running and thus falling down and getting hurt. These are not unusual happenings in the life of an adolescent, but after some experiences he adjusts himself properly. Some guardians fail to understand that such happenings are natural. They due to their lack of understanding rebuke or snub the adolescent. This kind of treatment makes the adolescent's life miserable.

Difference between the Strength of Boys and Girls

There is a difference between the strength of boys and girls. The bones and muscles of women are comparatively smaller than those of men. Therefore, boys have greater physical strength than girls. With the increase in age the physical strength in boys increases.

Skin and Hairs

The gentle and smooth skin of childhood becomes somewhat rougher and darker during adolescence. The skin of face and neck are greatly affected. With the appearance of pimples on nose, forehead and chin the skin on face becomes ugly. the colour of hair also changes and it become somewhat harder and darker.

INTERNAL PHYSICAL CHANGES

During adolescence internal changes also take place along with external ones. These changes influence the adolescent's behaviour significantly.

Heart

The shape and the size of heart greatly increases during adolescence. At the age of six years the heart develops four or five times more than what it was at the time of birth. At the age of 12 years, it is seven times bigger and at the age of 17 or 18 years it is twelve times larger than what it was at the time of birth. The veins as compared to heart develop less. During childhood there is always an apprehension of the heart getting easily tired. This fear disappears during adolescence. The beatings of the pulse decreases during childhood and further gets reduced during adolescence. The blood pressure in girls of ten to thirteen years of age is higher than that in boys. Then the blood pressure in boys steadily increases and after the age of 16 years it becomes higher than that in girls.

Lungs

With the onset of adolescence the speed of lungs development increases greatly. The development of lungs is intimately connected with the development of chest, because both develop simultaneously. The rate of respiration also decreases during adolescence as compared to that during childhood, but the inhaling, exhaling and retaining capacity of lungs increases. The lungs during middle adolescence are generally larger in boys than in girls. Before this stage the girls' lungs may be larger.

Digestive Organs

All digestive organs develop sufficiently during adolescence. The stomach gets larger and does not appear swelled even after taking food. The intestines increase in length and girth. The liver at this stage is 12 times larger than what it was at the time of birth.

Food

The adolescent needs more food of nutritious value because of developing limbs. During adolescence the boy's hunger increases. The adolescent generally take twice as much food as is taken by an adult. People are sometimes surprised to see the quantity of food consumed by an adolescent. When any uncharitable comment about his food comes to his knowledge he is disturbed and feels shy in eating food along with others. The adolescent have to suffer emotional shocks frequently. These shocks adversely affect his appetite. Consequently, his appetite sometimes becomes sharp and sometimes sluggish. Like pregnant women the adolescent also likes to eat various types of food. The adolescent is unable to observe discipline or control over his food habit. It is very trying for him to control his tongue in relation to eating. So he has no hesitation in eating what he gets. This habit occasionally affects his digestive system and he often suffers from eruptions in skin, pain in stomach or constipation.

Nervous System

The mind develops at a very fast pace during childhood. With the start of adolescence the mind reaches its maximum weight and all nerves related to it almost get developed. Due to all these developments and circumstances the mental development in an adolescent reaches the peak. It has also been observed that an adolescent's mental curiosities increases more than before. He develops thinking and reasoning power. Consequently, he takes more pleasure in mental work.

General Health

During adolescence the general health of boys and girls improve, because by this time they become free from common childhood diseases. However, if his surroundings are unhealthy he may develop seasonal diseases. Due to constipation he may develop indigestion, cold or headache. Here we have to note that the adolescent gets easily tired because of rapid speed of development of his body. His power of concentration slightly decreases. It is common for adolescents to suffer from indigestion and lack of appetite. This results in the shortage of blood in his body and he appears lean and yellowish. Anaemia or lack of blood is a disease with which girls suffer more than boys. At this age the boys generally complain of headache and the girls of pain in the waist. Doctors are of the view that adolescent who are socially and economically lowly placed are liable to contact tuberculosis. The health improves considerably by the time the adolescence is over.

Imaginary Diseases

An adolescent may appear to be suffering from imaginary diseases. He thinks it true when some one points out that his health is bad. This tendency is more prominent in girls. Some adolescents appear sickly when they are weak in school work, quarrel with friends and have family problems.

Neglect of Health

Generally, it is seen that adolescents do not care to observe rules regarding healthy living. They think that rules relating to health are absurd and they protest against them. They pay no attention to commonly recognised health practices during winter, summer and rains. They also violate recognised food practices. They eat in the market anything at any time. All this adversely affects their health.

PSYCHOLOGICAL SIGNIFICANCE OF PHYSICAL CHANGES

Craze for Building of Personality

Our mental attitude undergoes some change on the day when we have a hair cut or put on new clothes. On getting the hair cut we frequently see our face in the mirror and try to find out whether we are looking prettier after the hair cut. Similarly, after putting on new clothes we experience smartness and feel encouraged. By keeping this experience in mind we can imagine how much smartness and encouragement the adolescent must be feeling when his own personality was undergoing a tremendous change. During adolescence the individual completely changes. He is now an absolutely new personality. This new personality brings with it new ideas, desires and thinking. Consequently, he forms a new view towards the life as a whole. He gradually realises his importance. He feels that as compared with others he is not physically behind and in physical appearance he is on par with them. So he tries to get those rights which others enjoy. Every behaviour of the adolescent is motivated with this desire. He thus gets busy in building up his personality. In this process of personality building the standard of living, dress, etc., all play a prominent part. He now starts wearing clothes on the pattern of adults so that other may take him to be an adult.

Expectating Appreciations from Others

The adolescent starts taking pride over his various physical developments. He, however, does not understand that development during adolescence is a normal process. So he secretly entertains the desire that other should shower praise on him. Moved by this desire he takes part in organised games and sports. Those adolescents who due to any reason have not attained full physical development and are unable to participate successfully in organised games and sports develop a feeling of inferiority complex. Many boys consider themselves superior to girls because they think that they have more physical strength. They forget that their greater strength is due to their being a male and for that they need not take pride.

Fear of Criticism

The adolescent is very much afraid of adverse criticism because his physical development does not always take place according to his desire. He is afraid of pimples appearing on his face. Boys are more afraid of it, although girls may also suffer from it. Some girls and boys get so many pimples on their faces that they feel shy in appearing before others. They do not hesitate to use any medicine, lotion or powder to get rid of pimples. They are also in look out of advertisements for getting such medicines or powders.

No Uniformity in the Physical Development

The development process, during adolescence does not proceed on a uniform pattern. Sometimes some organs develop more and they look ugly in proportion to other organs. For instance, legs and arms develop more rapidly and appear very large in proportion to other limbs. The girls feel this very much and show reluctance in appearing before others because according to their concept of feminine beauty hands and legs should not be too long. They try to cover their hands as much as possible. Similarly, they also make efforts not to expose their legs before others. Boys also suffer from this complex, but girls show more concern.

Development of Nose

During adolescence the nose develops earlier than other limbs, so it appears disproportionate to other organs. Friends of the adolescent sometimes make unpsychological remarks about it. The adolescent also starts feeling more embarrassing and get worried. But when the face is fully developed the nose looks in proportion and the worry of adolescent disappears.

Shyness due to Individual Difference

In some adolescents the physical development takes place earlier and in some the process of development takes more time. Those in whom the process starts late feel inferiority complex before their friends. The adolescents whose voice turns hoarse have to face embarrassment because his associates point out to the defect in his voice. Both the boys and girls have to face this situation. Due to individual difference the degree of embarrassment and shyness experienced by the girls and boys may differ. Besides, the voice or any other physical deformity also creates embarrassing situation for the adolescents. This deformity is not so embarrassing during childhood, because, the child gets proper attention of his parents for the deformity. But the position changes during adolescence. Any thing which is unusual in the adolescent makes his position embarrassing.

Emotional Tension

It is not difficult for the adolescent to feel emotional tension. He is often in emotions of anger, pleasure or indifference. The adolescent is generally more emotional. He displays anger on flimsy grounds. People also taunt and pass remark over this kind of behaviour. This is very painful to him. He often vows not to speak such words which may injure the feelings of others. But he seldom succeeds in this attempt. This failure sometimes makes him think that he is incompetent.

SUMMARY

Physical changes in an adolescent are closely related with emotional, mental and social developments. If the physical development is not satisfactory all other developments are affected.

There are two methods of studying physical development. The first one is known as the 'Retest' method, while the second is named 'Sampling' method.

Physical development are both external and internal. In the external development the hands, legs, head, face, nose and chest etc., are included. These developments are visible. With the external development the adolescents personality develops and he looks more like an adult. By the end of adolescence, almost all external developments are complete. The boys and girls attain their full height and gain considerably in weight because their bones and muscles develop.

In the internal development come organs like heart, lungs, digestive organs and nervous system.

During this period the adolescent's behaviour undergoes complete change. He is generally indifferent towards recognised and established practices of building good health. He also feels that he is suffering from some diseases which are wholly imaginary.

During adolescence he tries to build his personality and expects appreciation of his achievements from others. He is also afraid of others' criticism. He also suffers from emotional tension and his feelings are easily injured.

Physical development of the various limbs and organs do not proceed uniformly. Some organs develop early, while others take longer time. For instance, nose, legs and arms develop earlier. There are individual differences in physical developments.

Exercises

1. What is the special significance of physical development during adolescence? How is the behaviour of the adolescent affected by it?
2. Describe the internal changes during adolescence.
3. Describe the external changes during adolescence and show how they are related with the behaviour of the adolescents.

Notes

1. Van Dyke G.E. The Effect of the Advent of Puberty on the Growth in Height and Weight of Girls.

4

Emotional Behaviour of Adolescents

Method of Studying Emotions of Adolescents

It is easy to study the emotional behaviour of an infant or a child, but it is difficult in case of an adolescent. During the period of infancy the individual is under the constant control or supervision of another person because he is weak and helpless in carrying out his activities. It is, therefore, easy to understand a stimulus and its responses in his case. The guardians may also tell many things about their behaviours. The children will also not object if the places of their activities and actions and reactions are watched. At this stage of life they do not possess any private life and, therefore, they do not object. The real difficulty is experienced in studying the emotional behaviour of adolescents because they do not want others to observe their behaviours which they claim as their private affairs. This kind of attitude on the part of adolescents affects their other emotional behaviours. Consequently, it is difficult to study any specific behaviour of the adolescent. It is, therefore, difficult to know the responses of an adolescent at the time of a specific emotion. Psychologists, therefore, prefer other methods to that of observation. But other methods do not yield reliable results. So help has to be taken from other methods. We shall describe below some of these methods :

Diary Method

In this method the adolescent boys and girls are asked to maintain a diary and record their feelings, emotional experiences and responses at different occasions. By studying these diaries psychologists try to reach certain conclusions. The defect in this method is that if the adolescent does not record the responses immediately, he generally forgets them. The second defect is that an individual seldom faithfully records his feelings. So we cannot fully rely on these diaries to reach a reliable conclusion.

Controlled Diary Method

More reliable results may be expected from controlled diary method. In this method the adolescent is required to immediately record his feelings pertaining to any situation. In this way, the chances of forgetting the facts and feelings are remote. Gates for the first time adopted this method in relation to the students of Bernard College for recording their emotional behaviours while under the influence of anger. In this method the individual is required to write for some days the date, time and intensity of emotional responses.

Questionnaire Method

In this method the adolescents are required to answer certain questions. The questions are so framed as to throw light on various emotional experiences undergone by them. Some questions are given below as samples :

1. What type of feelings come to your mind after seeing a man in some great trouble?
2. What are your feelings if an individual harms you unintentionally?
3. Who is your ideal a man or a woman?

ADOLESCENCE : A PERIOD OF STRESS AND STRAIN

Psychologists have defined adolescence as a period of stress and strain. However, they differ regarding the causes leading to this development. This stormy period begins from the middle of adolescence and lasts till the end of adolescence. In the previous chapter it has been indicated that physical changes and development greatly influence the emotions of adolescents. But it will not be proper to hold this change and development solely responsible for the stormy emotional phase in an adolescent's life. In fact, the real reason is the social environment. Had the social environment been patterned on a psychological base, the emotional condition of the adolescent would not have been so miserable. It is needless to remark that in the present condition of society, this kind of psychological approach is not possible. Perhaps it had never been possible in the past, nor would it be possible in future. Under such a situation, the adolescent cannot escape from falling a victim to emotional storms. As regards the depth of emotion, it will depend on different circumstances. In other words, we may say that difference lies in the degree and not in the kind.

Its Wide Influence

If the boy's emotion is not analysed properly and proper treatment is not given, he will surely be led away by emotions in the same way as water carries away a blade of grass. The adolescent's patience exhausts when he finds the social environment in opposition to his reasonable desires. This affects his behaviour and his activities in wrong directions. The effect of his emotional unrest is clearly visible in all his actions relating to family and society. He looks worried and short-tempered. It is not unusual for him to quarrel with others. The development of adolescent's personality depends to a large extent on his emotional life. Self-control and sympathetic attitude of well-wishers are very helpful in controlling the emotional storms of an adolescent. The sympathetic attitude of parents and guardians is necessary for a good development of adolescent's personality. In the absence of this sympathetic approach, the emotional difficulties of the adolescent are aggravated.

SPECIAL CHARACTERISTICS OF ADOLESCENT'S EMOTIONS

Violent Type

The emotional intensity of an adolescent differs from that of a child or adult. The child's emotional intensity comes all of sudden with full fury even on ordinary matters. Gradually, the child learns to control his emotions. In achieving this emotional control he is conscious of the approval or disapproval of the society. In fact, the approval or disapproval by the society serves as a criterion for his behaviour. Due to his physical changes and social environment the emotional fury appears in an adolescent. Due to these changes the society begins to expect more from the adolescent. In the beginning the adolescent is unable to fulfil these expectations of the society. Consequently he develops emotional tension. People start criticising him for this tension. The adolescent also realises his mistake, but it is not easy for him to control his emotions so early and easily. He feels ashamed for his failures because socially his emotional responses are condemnable.

Lack of Stability

The emotional intensity of an adolescent lacks stability. It is not difficult for an adolescent's emotion to touch extremes on both sides. For instance it may range from self-confidence to cowardice, from happiness to unhappiness or from deep love to intense hatred. Although instability is present in child's emotions too, but he seldom comes down from one extreme to another. The emotional intensity of a child is mostly related to his physical conditions. When the child is healthy and his necessary desires are fulfilled he appears happy. He does not then trouble others by his emotional fury. But adolescents differ in this respect. His emotional fury is mostly related to social things and it easily goes from one extreme to the other within a short time.

Lack of Control in Expression

The adolescent suffers from impatience. He lacks control in expressing his feelings. It is easy for him to say any thing when he is under the influence of an emotion. An adolescent may easily weep or laugh on flimsy grounds like children. Some guardians get worried over this development and think that the boy is developing a bad habit. But this notion is not correct. If an adolescent gets a favourable environment he succeeds in getting control over expression of his feelings by the end of adolescence. It is often observed that it becomes difficult for an adolescent to hide his feelings. If he feels happy over something his lips smile. In the same way when he is angry his eyebrows also change curves, flouts elders' orders or carries them out under protests. Expression of gloominess on the face, stopping speaking, refusing food, beating or snubbing children or servants indicate adolescent's lack of control over expression of his feelings. In a fit of emotional fury the adolescent takes oath secretly or openly not to do a certain work.

Emotional Fury Lasts Longer

As compared to children the emotional fury lasts longer in adolescents. The children's desires or feelings change rapidly, but not so of an adolescent. If he gets annoyed with anyone, the anger may last for a long period. Psychologists attribute it to the adolescent's effort to develop self-control. However, in this effort the adolescent succeeds in the other direction. Instead of controlling his emotion, he himself gets under its influence. Consequently, the effect of emotional fury lasts longer. If the adolescent starts considering himself socially free in giving vent to his feelings, the fury of emotion will not last long. Sometimes due to social traditions he finds himself utterly helpless and is unable to give expression to his emotions. In this situation the emotion continues to stay for days together. Under such an influence of emotion his interest in others gets diminished. Sad looks, discourtesy, avoiding others company are some of the indications of such a kind of emotion present in the adolescent.

Intense Thinking Under Emotional Influence

Under the influence of an emotion the adolescent remains buried in thoughts. This is not good for him. In this mood he sometimes thinks of running away from the house or thinks of committing suicide. The feeling of committing suicide is more common in girls because they are more sentimental. We often hear boys committing suicide after failing in examinations. Domestic disputes, disappointment in love affairs or failure in accomplishing a task etc., may also be causes behind the adolescent's attempted suicides. It is quite natural for the adolescents to indulge in some kind of day-dreaming. The guardians, therefore, need not worry on this account. But in order to properly channelise this day-dreaming, the environment around the adolescent should be educative and he should, occasionally, be given opportunities for the expression of his feelings.

Inspired by Sentiments

In the adolescents emotional fury a touch of sentiment is present. During early childhood the sentiments are limited to concrete objects, because the child mind is not developed to such a degree as to enable him to appreciate abstract ideas. The adolescent's mental development is of a higher order and abstract ideas come with his/this preview. An adolescent may appreciate abstract ideas and develop love for them. So he may develop sentiments for patriotism, beauty, love kindness, and sympathy etc. Thus his emotional fervour may have some sentiments.

CAUSES OF EMOTIONAL INTENSITY

Need for Re-adjustment

We have already remarked in the previous chapters that many revolutionary changes take place during adolescence. Due to these changes an adolescent has to develop many new habits so he has to readjust himself in the changed atmosphere and in order to achieve this he has to labour hard. He succeeds in this attempt upto some extent. In this attempt his emotional intensity is in proportion to success he achieves. In order to properly adjust himself and win praise from others he intentionally wants to develop certain habits but he does not know whether his attempt is in correct or wrong direction. Consequently, at times, his emotional intensity increases.

Feeling of Insecurity

It has been repeatedly mentioned earlier that the main cause of an adolescent's emotional intensity is social environment and not his physical changes. The adolescent has to struggle hard with his social environment because of his early childhood habits. He is no more a child and people expect from him behaviour of a mature person. The adolescent finds his position very insecure and uncertain in this struggle. He fails to know when some of his behaviours will be subjected to bitter criticism. Thus he always carries on an emotional tension. Now we shall understand the points that are related to the feeling of insecurity in adolescents.

Expecting an Adult's Behaviour

We have already said that people start expecting from adolescents behaviour worthy of an adult because in physical appearance they look like adults. This physical development takes hardly two to three years. But his habits are practically like those of a child. People also comment that his childishness has not yet disappeared. People who comment like this, forget their own adolescence. This uncharitable criticism is very painful to the adolescent and he is doubtful about the suitability of many of his behaviours. This increases his emotional intensity.

Curiosity in Boys and Girls

With advancement in age the curiosity of knowing each other increases in boys and girls. They are very curious to know how they should behave in each other's presence. This problem is easily solved in a family where there are brothers and sisters present, but if in the family such a condition does not exist, the adolescent needs readjustment. In the absence of proper satisfaction of this desire the emotional intensity persists in the adolescent.

Finding Himself Incompetent in Various Situations

The adolescent in many situations finds himself unequal to the occasion. For instance, he does not find it easy to enter college for the first time for pursuing studies or taking part in the proceedings of a meeting. He entertains a fear of committing mistakes. The effect of this fear is very telling. Sometimes out of fear he commits mistakes. Thus the fear of incompetence makes his life very miserable.

Failure in Studies

Some students are good at schools, but they find difficulties when they come to college. In the schools a boy has to depend much on his memory but in college studies reasoning takes the place of memory. Consequently, those boys whose reasoning is weak have to face difficulties in college life. This increases emotional intensity in them.

Non-Fulfilment of Desires

The emotional intensity of an adolescent increases if his desires remain unfulfilled. He desires to put on new clothes like his companions or wants to join some entertainment. But his economic condition stops him from doing so. It is natural for him to get emotionally disturbed in this situation. So whenever such a situation arises before him he gets emotionally perturbed. Besides, his parents or guardians also act as hurdle in his way when he tries to satisfy any of his wants. Their control also makes him emotionally perturbed at times.

Quarrels

We have hinted earlier that domestic quarrels create emotional intensity in adolescents. Besides, the quarrels of his friends also increase his emotional tension. Some adolescents always entertain the feeling that they are not treated properly. The strict control of parents and criticism of his activities compel him to entertain such feelings. Misbehaviour of friends also give him the feeling that injustice is being done to him. Consequently, he quarrels with them. It is then natural that emotional intensity overpowers him.

Strict Parental Control

Some parents think it necessary to keep their boys and girls under strict control. They do not rely on adolescent's growing wisdom. So they try to impose their advice in every work which the boys or girls undertake. The boys and girls resent it, though most of them do not dare to express this resentment openly. The adolescents, therefore, do not consider elders progressive and try to neglect their device. This situation creates emotional tension in adolescents.

Religious Doubts

The parents of some adolescents are religious minded and they want to bring their children according to their own religious traditions and principles. The problems of religious doubts are very rare during childhood, but they develop during adolescence. The adolescent's mental development by this time reaches a stage where he can follow somc aspects of religion. When he hears from his teachers and friends such things as go against the religious ideas of his parents he is mentally agitated and develops a mental tension.

Vocational Problems

A child under twelve is not worried about choosing a carreer but this is not the case with an adolescent. By the end of adolescence he is worried about his future career. In physical appearance he is like an adult so people expect him to earn his livelihood. The adolescent at this stage does not understand the profession he should choose for himself. If due to family troubles or bad financial condition he is compelled to join some profession early, his worries increase tremendously. This worry makes his life very miserable.

SOME EMOTIONS OF ADOLESCENTS

We have already stated in the previous pages that as compared to the methods of studies of a child's emotion the methods of studies of an adolescent's emotions are not very much reliable. We have also given the reasons for it and it is needless to repeat them here. However, psychologists, have attempted to study the behaviour of adolescents. We have already mentioned the methods of their study earlier. On the basis of these studies we shall discuss very briefly some of the more important emotions experienced by adolescents. The difference between the emotions of children and those of adolescents will also be hinted at in the following :

Worry

Worry is caused by imaginary ideas. It may be regarded as a kind of fear. The individual entertains fear because of some imaginary nature of some future happening. Imagination is deeply related to mental development. The child is comparatively less mentally developed, therefore, his imagination is of a lower order. He is, therefore, less worried as compared with adolescents. A young child may be often seen angry or unhappy but seldom worried because he is unconcerned with worldly affairs. His worry, therefore, is a temporary phase and unreal. Pinter and Lev[1] studied 500 children of New York city in relation to their worries. They found that their worries were confined generally to their family or school problems. They were not much worried from financial, health, social or personal problems.

Causes of Worry

The boys and girls sometimes appear worried during pre-adolescence. They are much worried about school work. Hicks and Hayes[2] have tried to prove it with the help of their experiments. The girls of 13 or 14 years appear worried about their work and appearance. According to Sakellariou, G.[3] the adolescent appear worried about his studies and future between the age of 12 and 14 years. Between 15 to 17 years he is worried about studies, future, love affairs and poverty. Between 18 to 22 years he is worried about marriage. It is generally seen that boys are comparatively more worried than girls in respect of earning money and acquiring more qualifications. This worry is deeply related to his capability. The boys mostly thinks all the time whether he will ever be able to earn sufficient money or not.

Fear

The emotion of fear is acquired on the basis of one's past experiences. Because it is acquired on basis of past experiences, therefore, individual variations are possible. The causes of fear vary with age. The fear in children are mostly due to the existing environment. The fear in an adolescent may be imaginary also. He starts fearing of the coming events. So some cause may be traced in his fear. The fear in a child may also be without any foundation. Generally, the cause of fear in his case relates to his personal problems. In the fear of adolescent social causes may also be present because he develops interest in social things and is conscious of appreciation and criticism of the society. Consequently, he is always afraid of doing things according to his desires. He tries to achieve success in his work and tries not to belie the expectations of others. As a result of this fear, the adolescent feels shy in presenting himself before others.

Causes of Fear in Adolescents

We may divide the fear in adolescent in three categories: (i) Relating to objects, e.g. tiger, snake, storm, sea or aeroplane etc. (ii) Social causes, e.g. sometimes the adolescent fears meeting strangers. He also fears the company of strangers or olders. It is also not strange that he may fear loneliness or crowd. He fears delivering speech or describing an object before others. Besides, these social causes there are certain other causes which may be regarded as personal. We may also call them 'general' because these causes may be traced both in young and old persons, e.g. poverty, dangerous ailment, fcar of becoming invalid, impotency, dismissal from service, defamation, failure in examination, marriage, immorality or actions causing distress to parents. An adult may also be afraid of these things.

Relation of Fear with Development

Fear is closely related to development. With the advancement of age an individual develops understanding and reasoning. The fear also decreases in proportion to the development of his development. Viewed in this angle 'fear' is an indication of our mental immaturity and ill health. With the development of understanding an individual learns proper way of behaving in a particular situation. Similarly, with the increase in reasoning power he understands the causes relating to any happening. Consequently, he gets tough and gradually throws out fear from his mind. An adolescent who earlier entertained fear on account of his lack of understanding roots out fear on attaining understanding. If an adolescent who is afraid of water is taught swimming with love and sympathy, his fear of water will gradually disappear. The boy who suffers from inferiority complex may do great work if a feeling of self-confidence is instilled in him. The self-confidence acquired in one sphere may be helpful in driving out fear in other spheres. All this is directly related to age. All these things cannot be taught at a time. The adolescents should get rid or many fears by the end of adolescence. By this time he should develop self-confidence, self-dependence, necessary ability to succeed or face various social situations successfully as also the ability to understand programmes of future and execute them with individual and social angles successfully. Needless to remarks that guardians owe a lot of responsibility in this respect towards the adolescents. The adolescent's personality may be well developed by creating a psychological atmosphere around him.

Jealousy

Jealousy is social in outlook. It is born of anger. It is commonly observed that the object which at one time is loved by a man turns into an object of hatred and jealousy. A very common instance of this kind of jealousy may be seen in those persons who love a child but the child only loves his father and mother. Such persons then start hating the very child on whom they earlier bestowed their full attention and affection. The child also entertains a feeling of jealousy against his school-mates in relation to studies and sports. This is also witnessed in adolescents. Adolescents are attracted towards the opposite sex. Boys are attracted towards girls and *vice-versa*. The adolescents get enraged and disturbed if due to social restrictions they find it difficult to satisfy this desire. If there is a rival in this field the adolescent loses his temper and is ready to fight the rival in the same way as children fight among themselves in order to win something. This kind of behaviour on the part of the adolescent is unsocial, so efforts should be made to check it. Mostly, the adolescent expresses his jealousy vocally but it will not be surprising if he assaults the rival.

Anger

There is no vital difference between the types of anger entertained by a child and those by an adolescent. The difference lies in their different situations, actions and time. The child gets angry when he finds obstacles in fulfilment of his natural desires. He possesses no knowledge about the morality or immorality of his desire. The cause of anger in an adolescent is mostly social. The adolescent may get angry on being harassed, compelled to do a work against his will, taunted or when a work is not accomplished according to his liking. The adolescent girls get angry when hurdles are placed in the fulfilment of their desires, when sarcastic remarks or taunts are passed against them or when they are insulted. When not getting an opportunity of expressing his feeling, the adolescent gets enraged. He then suffers a great mental agony.

Reactions of Adolescents and Children Differ

During anger the reactions of children are confined to their body's organs. The angry child stiffens his hands and feet. When placed in lap he stiffens his whole body. His face turns red and he starts weeping. He may also show other reactions according to the stage of his development. In adolescents the reactions to anger are different. When harassed he says unpleasant things to his tormentor. He is also not tired in condemning him before others. He never lets go any opportunity of letting him down. He appears restless in anger. He may also tear or destroy objects during anger. He stops speaking. The return of normalcy in adolescent's mood depends on the intensity of anger. Sometimes the adolescent shows his contempt to an offender for a considerable period. He vows within his heart not to see him again in future.

Envy

The cause of envy is personal. The child on seeing others' good dress or house may feel envious. In this way we see that envy is related to some desired object. The element of envy is very meagre in children. If it is present it is easily pacified. If a child entertains envy on seeing another child wearing new dress his envy may then be pacified by giving him, too, any new garment. He will not show impertinence for taking the same type of garment. Any new garment will satisfy him. The reason is that he is not yet in a position to determine its value. But this is not the case with the adolescent. He understands the value of an object. He is determined to fully compete with his rival. He will not be satisfied by any garment except the type which his rival wears.

Vocal Reactions

Reactions relating to envy are mostly vocal. The adolescent passes remarks or expresses his displeasure in clear words. An adolescent girl on seeing other wearing fine ornaments may criticise or condemn the ornaments or she may say that she does not like to wear those types of ornament.

Annoyance

Annoyance is not as troublesome as anger. Of course, it disturbs the mind for some time. According to Cason[4] people get annoyed on seeing others peculiar behaviour. Some people take pleasure in annoying others. In fact, the individual who gets easily annoyed invites others to make him annoyed more and more. Due to some personal ideas an individual is prone to get annoyed with certain peculiar behaviour of others. The tendency of getting annoyed is less in adolescents. The grown ups or aged persons generally get annoyed when they see any behaviour which appears peculiar to them. This tendency does not change easily and persists for a long time.

Curiosity

The element of curiosity is strong during childhood. Under its influence the child gets busy in destroying or building an object. With mental development the standard of curiosity in the child gets developed and he starts asking a series of questions. Consequently, he is snubbed and many of his curiosities die. Due to this treatment in childhood the tendency of curiosity becomes dull during adolescence. So during adolescence the environment should be colourful at times in order to stimulate the process of mental development in the desired direction.

Desire to know Matter Regarding Sex

We have already remarked that during adolescence boys and girls have a curiosity to know each other. Due to various physical changes they particularly develop curiosities to know thing related to each other's body. They, therefore, show keen interest in talking about these matters with others. They look into sex books in order to satisfy this desire. This feature is found both in boys and girls.

Other Curiosities Depend on Environment

Besides the desire to know sex-matters the adolescent also is attracted towards scientific inventions, moral and religious problems and international affairs. But the development of these curiosities depend on his environmental surroundings. If the environment lacks educational colour it is possible that the adolescent may not be attracted towards these subjects. Sometimes the adolescent simply puts questions to elders only to show his knowledge. Such adolescents tend to become indolent and develop the habit of side-tracking the real issues. If he is offered advice to read a particular book in order to satisfy his curiosity he will start offering excuses.

Affection

The child is very grateful to others. If some good is done to him he wants to pay it back immediately. He starts loving anyone who gives him joy. He even develops affection with his lifeless toy. Evidently, he does not bases his love on reason. This is not the case with adolescents. He bases his affection on reason. It is not usual with him to start loving anyone without reason. His circle of friends is limited. It is limited to family, near relations, friends or class-fellows. The adolescent's emotion is deeper than that of a child. Therefore, an adolescent's affection is more lasting than that of a child's. If the adolescent loves someone, he tries to establish nearness with him. He feels hurt if this relationship is not established. The child express his affection through laughter, cry, pat or by offering to be kissed. But the expression of affection in an adolescent is more controlled. He wants to reach his object of affection and tries to do something for it.

Delight

Delight in an adolescent, like the child, depends to a large extent on good physical health, although for delight things relating to environment besides good health are also needed. According to psychologists possession of good health may give various types of delight in four different situations. The first situation is that of an environment according to an individual's abilities. If the environment does not give full scope for the expression of his abilities he will not be able to exploit it fully and therefore will not get delight and will also not be able to get people's appreciation. For instance if the adolescent does not have a sharp memory and had been admitted to a reputed college, he may not then be able to enjoy his classes and instead of being delighted he may develop anger, contempt and jealousy.

Ability to Catch Wit

The other situation is related to wit or humour. The adolescent should possess ability to recognise the element of humour during conversation. Without this ability he will not be able to enjoy humour and will not feel delighted. This ability will depend on intellect, education and environment of the adolescent. Some people lack this power to a large extent and consequently most of the time appear sad. It is easy to laugh on the actions of others, but difficult to do so on one's own action. The adolescent, to prove his superiority easily laughs over others, but if somebody else laughs at him he feels deeply hurt.

Unexpected Situation

The third situation is that one when he unexpectedly instead of experiencing unhappiness experiences happiness. For instance, in a match seeing a clear defeat unexpectedly turning into victory, the adolescent feels highly delighted and gets into a hearty laughter.

Feeling of Superiority

The fourth situation is that one when the adolescent experiences a feeling of some kind of superiority. We have mentioned earlier that the adolescent feels mostly hurt when he comes across his own criticism. So he is delighted when he hears of his superiority. For example, topping in the examinations, being getting elected as president in a meeting or hearing appreciation from a teacher delights him.

Easy Realisation of the Feeling of Delight

The feeling of delight in an adolescent may easily be experienced. Delight makes him smile. His eyes take full view of others. The adolescent may laugh heartily instead of smiling. The intensity of his laughter depends on the depth of his joy.

FACTORS INFLUENCING EMOTIONAL LIFE

The emotional life of everyone does not run on the same line because each person differs from the other. We shall describe below some factors which are responsible for influencing an adolescent's or of any one's different emotional experiences.

Indifferent Health

The human being easily falls victim to some or the other emotion if he is having indifferent health. A weak man easily gets irritated. He also gets irritated when tired. Everyone is aware how unbalanced a person becomes emotionally during illness. The healthy man more successfully controls his emotions and his behaviour appears disciplined.

Women More Emotional but Men Easy Victims of Emotional Rage

It is generally observed that as compared to men, women are more emotional. They are easily overpowered by emotions. They start weeping, laughing or get angry easily. Researches have not yet been able to establish whether it is the result of environment or hereditary qualities. But some researches have proved that after the end of adolescence and on attaining maturity women comparatively develop the ability to control emotions more than men because they need this quality in larger measures in life. Meltzer[5] found in his studies that male students of a college displayed anger 39 per cent more than the girls. These results go against the traditionally prevalent views. Stratton[6] also observed that men display more anger than women.

Intelligence

Psychologists have not yet made enough investigations for finding the nature of relationship between intelligence and emotional intensity. According to the researches of Meltzer[7] the intensity of anger varies according to difference in intelligence. Boys of superior intellect show more anger and they also argue more during anger.

Days of the Week

Some American psychologists have tried to find out if there exists any relationship between various days of the week and emotional intensity. Whether there is a difference in the behaviour of an individual on Monday, that is, when he attends work after enjoying the holiday on Sunday, and on Saturday after putting in five days of work. The names of Gates[8] and Meltzer are particularly worth mentioning as regards research on this subject. However, we do not find definite conclusions from their researches. So it is unnecessary to discuss them here.

Day Time

Smaller children show emotional intensity when hungry or thirsty or before retiring to bed. Gates observed that even adolescents display emotional intensity when hungry. It is not uncommon with them to show anger, regret or disappointment in evening when tired after the day's work.

EFFECT OF EMOTION

Appearance of emotion is as natural as the act of respiration. Emotion has both darker and brighter sides. But keeping all things in view there is more likelihood of harm from emotions. So it is necessary to keep them in check. We shall discuss below the effect of emotions on adolescents :

Source of Energy and Inspiration

The adolescent after working throughout the day gets tired and needs rest. Eating and sleeping merely do not provide him the desired rest. He, therefore, wants some of enjoyment. The emotion of delight removes his fatigue and he gets fresh for the work. Besides, emotions like fear, anger, affection and curiosity inspire him from time to time and through them he often works amazingly. This inspiration also instils in him the required energy.

Loss of Physical Power

Emotions like anger, worry and fear adversely affect the body. Under the influence of these emotions the individual suffers from loss of sleep. The adolescent gets tired in the morning. Neither he feels appetite nor does he eat to his heart's content. Consequently, he grows weak and thin. If efforts are not made in time to control these emotions the result will be the total loss of physical power and maladjustment of individual's nature.

Loss of Mental Power

Under the influence of intense emotion the power of reasoning declines and the adolescent loses his discretion. He does not know how to face the situation. He forgets to recall past experiences. It becomes difficult for him to concentrate on a subject. The greater the intensity of the emotion the weaker gets the adolescent. We see that a balanced person acts intelligently. He is equipped with enough energy and intelligence to execute a task. An individual loses his energy and discretion when over-powered by an emotion. Moor[9] observed in his studies that anger and fear greatly affect an adolescent's thinking process and he finds himself unable to concentrate on thinking about a subject. Perhaps the readers will also agree with Moor on the basis of their own experiences.

SUMMARY

It is easier to study emotions of a child, but not so of an adolescents. There are many methods to study emotional intensity and the important ones are : (i) The observation method, (ii) Diary method, (iii) Controlled Diary method, and (iv) Questionnaire method.

Psychologists have called the adolescent stage as a period of stress and strain and it has some special characteristics. These characteristics are the : (i) violent type, (ii) lack of stability, (iii) lack of control in expression, (iv) emotional fury lasting for a long period, (v) indulgence in intense thinking, and (vi) inspiration from sentiments.

The causes of emotional intensity may be traced in the need for readjustment, feeling of uncertainty and insecurity, expecting an adult's behaviour, mutual curiosity in boys and girls, finding himself incompetent in various situations, failure in studies, non-fulfilment of desires, quarrels, strict parental control, religious doubts and vocational problems.

The adolescent's experience many emotions. The main emotions faced by them are : (i) worry, (ii) fear, (iii) jealousy, (iv) anger, (v) envy, (vi) annoyance, (vii) curiosity, (viii) affection, and (ix) delight.

Some factors influence the emotional life of an adolescent. The main factor is bad health. Although women are more emotional, yet men fall easy victims to emotional rage. Intelligence, weekly days, different times of the day also influence emotional life.

Emotional intensity both beneficial and harmful to the individual, but generally the darker side has a slight edge over the brighter one. Emotion is, on the one hand, a source of energy and inspiration but on the other hand, it also harms the physical and mental power.

Exercises

1. What are the various methods of studying emotions of an adolescent?
2. What are the special characteristics of an adolescent's emotions?
3. What are the causes of emotional intensity ?

4. Describe any three emotions of an adolescent.
5. What are the factors that generally influence an adolescent's emotional experiences ?

Notes

1. Pinter R. and Lev J., "Worries of School Children" *J. Gene. Psychol.*, 56, 67-76.
2. Hicks G.A and Hayes, M. "Study of the Characteristics of 250 Junior High School Children", *Child Development.* 9, 219-242..
3. Sakellariou, G. "Anxieties and Complexes of Greek Youth."
4. Cason, H. 'Common Annoyance'.
5. Meltzer, H. 'Students' Adjustment in Anger', *J. Soc. Psychol.*, 4, 285, 308, 1933.
6. Stratton, G.M. 'Emotion and the Incidence of Disease' *J. Abnorm. Soc. Psychol.* 21, 19-23, 1933.
7. Meltzer H. 'Anger Adjustments in Relation to Intelligence and Achievement.' *J. Genet. Psychol.* 50, 63 - 82, 1937.
8. Gates G.S. 'An Observation Study of Anger', *J. Exp. Psychol.* 9, 325-326, 1926.
9. Moor H.T. 'Laboratory Tests of Anger, Fear and Sex Interest', *Amer J. Psychol.*, 28, 390-395, 1919.

5

Personal Interests of Adolescents

It is generally observed that an adolescent displays great enthusiasm in a work at early stages and sometimes he also goes out of way in executing the task. The same thing also holds good as far as his personal interests are concerned. Below we shall see that an adolescent even overlooks every thing else in pursuing his interests. But it will not be proper to base conclusions on the future of adolescents on the basis of these personal interests. By the end of the adolescent stage the individual starts developing some emotional stability. His permanent interests may be correctly guaged only after he attains emotional stability. However, the study of personal interests of adolescents cannot be overlooked because these greatly affect their character and personality. Below we come to this study :

Entirely Self-Centred

We have stated earlier that the adolescent starts thinking himself as an entirely new person because of his physical development. He forms a new opinion about himself. He desires that others consider him as a fully grown up individual and treat him accordingly. In order to get this treatment both adolescent boys and girls put on such dresses and adopt such modes of conversation which may attract others. Consequently, the adolescent devotes much of his time in establishing his individual identity. He is self-centred. He is ready to do everything for his progress and development. He is full of enthusiasm. This enthusiasm is found both in boys and girls. At this stage he prefers things personally related to him and does not care much about national or international topics. By the end of adolescence, he begins to take interest in social, national and international problems. Stoltz and other writers say that during adolescence :

> "The girls tries to show that she is equipped with all feminine qualities, whereas the boy wants to show that he possess all

qualities of a grown-up man. Consequently the girls spend most of their time in making their appearance more attractive. In order to impress others of their beauty they pay more attention in keeping their body clean and also try to make their style of speech and manners attractive. The boys try to prove their masculine qualities by competing in games and sports."[1]

INTERESTS REGARDING CLOTHES

Desire to Wear Clothes like Grown-ups

In the preceding pages it has been indicated that an adolescent is keen in being considered as an adult. This desire is present equally in boys and girls. In their effort to pose as grown-up their attention goes first towards their clothes. The boy wants to put on suit, hat, good shoes etc. He wants his clothes to be clean and well pressed. Similarly the adolescent girl tries to copy the elder women in the family. Children are indifferent in this respect. Their only desire remains to wear new and colourful dresses. They do not pay attention to prevailing fashions, as adolescents do.

Desire to Dress the Body

Children love deep colours. So they feel very happy when they put on such clothes. With the beginning of adolescence their interest in deep colours starts vanishing. During the middle adolescence their tastes become similar to those of adults. An adolescent wants to put on good dresses and make his appearance more attractive. The girls are comparatively ahead of boys in this respect. The girls want in addition to put on jewellery also. Under the influence of this desire they sometimes overlook the current fashion but gradually they revert back to the prevailing fashion.

Care for Accepted Social Traditions

In regard to dress, the adolescent boys and girls are inclined to abide by the current social conventions. They do not want to be criticised for their dress. According to psychologists the adolescent is very careful about his dress. His dress is intimately related to his ability, comfort and self-confidence. He may lack self-confidence if his dress is not in accordance with the current fashion. He considers other boys or girls in good dress superior to himself. Some boys want to hide their poverty through dresses.[2] Barr[3], in his studies, has observed that in the selection of dress the adolescent gives preference to the prevailing fashion over his personal comforts.

INTEREST IN SELF-APPEARANCE

The adolescent is very conscious about his appearance. He wants to display his body in the best possible manner. He considers it an important medium of commanding others respect. He realises the importance of the relationship between social achievements and his personal appearance. So the indifferent attitude of childhood starts changing. It is commonly observed that children do not pay much attention towards cleaning their hands, nails, face or other parts of the body. But during the adolescent stage, girls and boys are very particular about keeping themselves clean. During adolescence the boys and the girls start getting interest in each other. They therefore want to make their personal appearance as attractive as possible and they are even ready to stake everything to achieve this objective.

Attention on Body Built

In order to make his appearance attractive the attention of the adolescent first goes towards the built of his body. If his body is not developed according to his desire, he feels unhappy. The short-statured boys want to become tall and those who are weak want to become healthy. Those adolescent who grow tall feel depressed being lean and thin. They vow to make their body proportionate and strong but how far they succeed in giving a practical shape to their vow is another matter. They mostly take this vow under emotional moments. According to the current standard of health a fat body is not considered good. So fat boys and girls try to reduce their weight through dieting or exercise.

Efforts to remove Bad Body Odour

The adolescent becomes sensitive about the odour emanating from his body. Some change in the odour of body also takes place with physical changes. This change is particularly noticeable in the odour coming out of arm pits. A strange smell comes out of a girl's body, bring menses due to which she avoids sitting with others. The adolescent also thinks that foul smell comes out of one's mouth when he takes onions or garlics. He is worried to stop the foul odour from his body because he thinks that he will not get respect from his companions due to this foul smell. He, therefore, resorts to the use of different soaps and cosmetics advertised in papers. He also becomes particularly keen on keeping the body and the clothes neat and clean and it becomes a daily routine in his life.

Worries Relating to Face

Some people occasionally talk about the attractiveness or ugliness of the face. The adolescent listens to these remarks very carefully and he gets worried if he notices something ugly on his face. But the worst aspect of this subject is that there is no remedy to this worry because the face cannot be changed. If the nose is longish or flat it will continue to remain as such. However, adolescent's worry on this count cannot be brushed aside. If small pox had left its marks on the face the adolescent suffers from some inferiority complex. According to the prevailing conception of beauty the eyes should be big and lips thin. The adolescent looks in mirror and compares his eyes and lips with the prevailing beauty standard.

Sensitive about Skin Colour

The colour of the skin is also a factor determining one's beauty. The people with dark colour are not considered beautiful. Besides other necessary qualities, the fairer the colour of the skin the more beautiful an individual is considered to be. Black or dark complexioned girls try to show themselves more neat and clean. So powder becomes an essential cosmetic for them. Some boys also spend enough money on powders. Despite opposition from guardians, the adolescents continue their search for good cosmetics.

Hair Style

Style of the hair counts a lot and adolescents spend much time in combing their hairs. They want to adopt the latest style in dressing their hairs. They also see advertisements and enquire about their hair styles from their colleagues.

Moustache, Beard and Hairs on Hands and Legs

The boy appears to be happy to the moustache and beard appearing on his face because that indicates his masculine qualities, but if unfortunately the girl finds hairs on her face she gets exceedingly worried because hairs on face, hands and legs reduce one's beauty. She, therefore, tries to remove them through various means.

Nails

Adolescents are very particular in keeping their nails clean. The girls are extremely particular in taking care of their nails and beautifying them through different sheds of nail polish.

Efforts to Sweeten Hoarse Voice

A child's voice is generally sweet although he often cries and the voice may appear harsh. In the case of adolescents the voice starts getting hoarse and husky. Changes also occur in the voice of girls when they enter adolescence, but this change is not so ugly as it is in the case of boys, and the boys feel very shy on account of this development. The boy desires that the old sweetness of his voice may return, but this remains an unfulfilled dream. He considers his hoarse voice a defect in his personality. The notion settles down in his heart that others try to give undue attention to his voice. So he tries to give a twist or change to his voice, but he seldom succeeds in this effort.

INTEREST IN EXPRESSING FEELINGS

An adolescent is very much interested in expressing his feelings through lengthy letters, poems, stories and dramas. He is not worried about the quality of the matter he produces. He experiences great relief in writing them. These writings, though not indications of his merit, yet give a glimpse of the development of his merit in stages. Some adolescents also take to diary writing. Maintaining a diary is a very good source of letting out one's emotions. Many personal problems may be solved through this method. These diaries of adolescents are very interesting and are a good source of knowing their tastes and mental dispositions. They also give an idea of their future programmes. The adolescent does not feel shy in comparing his feelings with those of grown up men. But the tendency to give expression to one's feelings is not present in all adolescents. Some are very lazy in writing and some even do not know writing. For obvious reasons such adolescents feel great disappointment.

INTEREST IN LIFE'S FUTURE PROGRAMMES

Although in their play the children act as soldiers, doctors, engineers, judges etc., yet they think little about their future programmes. These offices appear attractive to them but many parents and guardians thinking that their wards are not experienced enough to decide upon their future career themselves undertake this responsibility. They decide what their son or daughter should become in future. As regards girls the parents have less to worry because they get married and their problem is solved, but the problem of a boy is different and serious and parents have to be on guard. They even overlook the taste and aptitude of their sons.

The parents try to choose the future career of their sons according to their own aptitude and liking. Younger children accept the decision of their parents because the power of reasoning and using discretion has not then developed sufficiently in them but the case of the adolescent is otherwise. He finds himself in an indecisive state of mind and does not know whether he should act according to the advice of his parents or according to his own aptitude. His future career hangs precariously at this stage and a wise decision only ensures a successful career.

Difficult to Decide about Future Profession

There are numerous openings before an adolescent. But he finds it difficult to choose a profession for his future and is worried about this. He realises that each profession calls for certain qualities of head and heart. So he tries to prepare himself mentally and physically for a particular profession. But he does not know about his aptitude and capabilities. He, therefore, occasionally gets nervous and worried. Now-a-days for every profession a definite training is necessary.

Therefore it is not easy for an adolescent to work in a profession for some time and find out his aptitude correctly.

ECONOMIC PROBLEM

Financial condition poses many difficulties before an adolescent and acts as a hurdle in choosing the correct profession. Adolescents need money to satisfy their desires or to pursue their studies for the profession of their choice. He, therefore, becomes desperate to earn money and takes up any job that comes in hand regardless of his aptitude. Sometimes despite knowing his aptitude correctly, he is not confident of his abilities. Often in order to attain economic independence he joins a lucrative job regardless of his aptitude. He also thinks that by being economically independent he can get himself counted among adults. There is already a latent desire in him to be treated as an adult and, therefore, he accepts willingly any job that comes in his way.

Sex Difference in choosing a Profession

An adolescent has to be very careful in choosing a profession because he wants to work throughout his life according to his taste, but this is not the problem with girls in India. The question of joining a profession seldom arises before a girl. However, the times are fast changing in the country and some girls either due to their aptitude or circumstances are compelled to seek some jobs and they are naturally worried. The girls like to choose such a career which may provide them physical security, less physical labour and peaceful environment. They do not like transferable jobs. They like such professions as, teaching, medical profession and nursing. Boys on the contrary are more enterprising and often go for professions which are beyond their abilities. Girls do not act in this manner. They are less ambitious and they only go for such work as they feel they can do easily. Mostly they are afraid of competition and, therefore, after joining one job they do not generally try to change over to another. Boys, generally prefer such jobs where they can issue orders to others, but the nature of girls differ in this respect.

Difficult to Choose a Profession

Most of the boys have to face the problem of choosing some

profession during adolescence although there are some who decide about their future professions during childhood and do not change their decision. Such adolescent experience a lot of relief but an overwhelming majority have to face this problem during adolescence. Some take to a profession for a short time without giving any serious thought to it. In such decisions either they copy a friend or follow the advice of their teachers or guardians. Such adolescents soon change over to another profession because aptitude also undergoes change with other developments. However, by the end of adolescence, a boy is in a position to deliberate seriously about choosing a permanent profession, because by then he is able to know the pros and cons of a decision and also about the strong and weak points of a profession. At this stage it becomes easier for the adolescent to take a decision, but sometimes a new problem of indecisiveness arises by too much knowledge of a particular profession and he goes on postponing the decision. Anyhow he finds himself compelled to take to a profession due to the pressure of others.

Influence of Friends and Family

Choosing of a profession is not a simple process because many things influence it. Among these the family and friends are main influences. In the early stage of adolescence it is the members of the family who exercise influence. Later on when he becomes more independent he leans towards friends for advice. In this way members of the family and friends exercise influence at times. Some boys prefer to be guided by their teachers in this respect, while many prefer to join the family profession.

DESIRE OF SELF-EXPRESSION AND COMMANDING RESPECT A PROMINENT FACTOR

Expressing himself is a natural human desire and the individual has this weakness since his gaining of consciousness. A child tries to win other's appreciation. This desire is also present in the adolescent. This desire influences the choosing of a profession and some adolescent strongly desires to choose a profession which may give him an opportunity to show his merits, such as, some business, medical practice, railway service, air service or some other professions. The desire of choosing such a profession is very strong, during childhood but some change takes place when the boy reaches the middle adolescence. He now wants to join a profession which may give him money and respect in society. He is ready to do any thing for commanding respect. So this feeling plays an important role in choosing a profession at the end of adolescence.

Desire to help others Instable

There is a desire to earn and extend help to others during later adolescence and this desire also influences the choosing of a profession, but it disappears soon. The adolescent considers it honourable to help others, but later on he becomes somewhat selfish in this respect and wants to take up only such professions which may give him more money.

Stability of Aptitude

It is needless to remark that development influences the choice of a profession. During adolescence the aptitude relating to profession undergoes changes with the development of knowledge and abilities. With the reaching of maturity the aptitude for a profession also gets stabilised. According to Strong[4] an individual develops stability of aptitude relating to profession toward adulthood.

DESIRE FOR INDEPENDENCE

Disobeying the Elders

The desire of independence is present even during childhood, but it becomes very strong during adolescence and the individual tries to become independent and break the control exercised by the parents and teachers. He wants to act freely and do as he wishes. He desires that others should recognise his independent personality. How to get this desire fulfilled becomes a problem to him. Now he thinks that he should learn all those things for which he has to depend on others and develop the faculty of taking a decision whenever necessary. Otherwise he cannot become independent. But all this quality is not developed immediately because its development takes time. The adolescent experiences many hurdles in his way of reaching independence. He finds the control exercised by his parents and teachers as main hurdles. The parents do not want to relax their control because they still think that adolescents are just like young children. The adolescent, on his part, resents it and thinks that others do not give him due recognition. Although adolescents want others' help but they do not want them to exercise control over them. If unfortunately the parents happen to be strict, the adolescents then start disobeying them. They disregard them and lean towards their friends for advice which in turn creates resentment in the parents who start adopting more adamant attitude.

Seeking Advice from Outsiders

A peculiar situation arises when an adolescent does not want to remain under the control of his parents and yet desires help from them. If the parents happen to be unsympathetic towards him, he starts seeking other people's advice. These outsiders are mostly the well-wishers of the family and although they tender advice, yet they are not in a position to compel the adolescent to act accordingly. The adolescent, however, feels happy in taking outsider's advice, because then they are free from parent's control.

Quarrel with Parents — Its Causes

The adolescent at times wants to severe off all relations with his parents because of their strict control. He, therefore, occasionally quarrels with them which leads to an unhappy family life. He also thinks to run away from home and sometimes actually runs away for a short period. The main reasons behind his quarrel with parents in either returning home late or beating younger brothers or sisters or disobeying the wishes of the parents. However, the desire to achieve independence is always at the background of these family quarrels.

Results of Getting or not Getting Freedom

The adolescent does not want to give any explanation about his conduct to his parents. He considers on explanation as an obstacle in his independence. However, despite having strong desire to get freedom, he fails in securing it. First of all, parents act as a big check in his efforts to get freedom. Secondly even if he gets it he is not mature enough to use it properly because he lacks confidence in his ability. He, therefore, gets frequent emotional tensions even if he succeeds in getting freedom. This adversely affects his personality.

Some parents are unwise enough in not allowing reasonable freedom to their adolescent children. They do not realise the deep relationship between adolescent's freedom and his feeling of self-respect. Those parents who interfere in routine affairs of adolescent lose respect in their eyes. The adolescent also thinks that he is being treated improperly. He gets sad and loses self-confidence.

DAY-DREAMS

All normal adolescents indulge into day-dreams and those who do not are generally below average in intelligence. Their day-dreams are related to their tastes and the more deeply one thinks the more submerged he gets into different kinds of day-dreams. The adolescents make castles in air regarding their future in these day-dreams. This holds good both with boys and girls. The day-dreams are both happy and unhappy according to their ideas. For instance, if he dreams of some kind of success he is happy and if he dreams of any failure he is naturally unhappy. During early adolescence the day-dreams are mostly happy ones. In the middle the day-dreams are full of tragic ideas. They suffer frustration, worry, fear and discouragement. The reason perhaps is that during the middle adolescence he is struggling to get freedom from parental control. Day-dreams consume much of adolescent's time. He is so engrossed in day-dreams that he forgets many things. However, it will not be correct to consider day-dreams as harmful. They are a source of inspiration to adolescents. They sometimes get immense help from day-dreams which may give new ideas to them and they may thus be able to achieve some constructive ideas in the realms of art and science. However, it has also its darker side inasmuch as if he remains engrossed in day-dreams abnormally, he deviates from the path of realities of life.

SUMMARY

During adolescence some personal interests become prominent. His entire attention is centred round his own person and he tries to pose as an adult and desires that others may treat him accordingly. He tries to speak, walk and dress like adults. He tries to show the finer points of his body and tries to appear attractive. This is true in the case of both boys and girls. They also pay attention to accepted norms of the society in order to escape criticism by others.

Both the boys and girls pay extra-ordinary attention to their body and physical appearance. They try to remain neat and clean, use cosmetics to remove foul body odour and make efforts to brighten their complexion. They adopt various hairstyles in order to appear more handsome. They also try to sweeten their voice which become hoarse at the onset of adolescence.

Another important feature is that they try to give expression to their personality through writing letters, stories, dramas, poems or diary.

One of their main problem is to achieve independence. They try to become economically independent of their parents, and also come out of their strict control. This sometimes leads to unfortunate quarrels with the parents. This is also the time for them to choose a profession according to their aptitude. At the age of 25 years they become mature enough to have a stable aptitude for a particular profession.

Adolescence is an age of day-dreaming for all. This is a natural process and helpful in developing one's thinking power. But too much of day-dreaming is harmful, because it leads away the adolescent from realities of life.

Exercises

1. Describe the major personal interests of adolescents.
2. Describe the hurdles that an adolescent faces in choosing his life profession.
3. What is the nature of day-dreamings as generally indulged into by adolescents ?
4. How does the mind of an adolescent work towards establishing his own individuality? Describe the difficulties that he encounters in this process.

Notes

1. Stoltz H.R., Jones K.C. and Chaffee, J. 'The Junior High School Age', Univ. high sch. F, Calif., 15, 63-72, 1937.
2. Hurlock, E.B. 'Motivation in Fashion', *Arch. Psychol*, N.Y., No. III, 1929.
3. Barr, E.P. 'A Psychological Analysis of Fashion Motivation', *Arch. Psychol.* N.Y., No. 171, 1934.
4. Strong, E.K. *Change in Interest With Age*, Standard University, Calif., Standard University Press, 1931.

6

Social Interests of Adolescents

Study of Social Interest for Correct Guidance

The study of interests of adolescents is necessary to correctly understand their behaviour and deal with them in a psychological manner. This proper understanding may help in removing the causes of frictions in the family. It is very necessary for parents and guardians to properly appreciate the interests of their children for the sake of their future career. On the other hand, it will reduce the tension in the boy's mind because he experiences satisfaction when he gets work according to his interests. The adolescent should, therefore, be given ample opportunity for his full and unfettered development through a correct appreciation of his interests. We have already mentioned in the preceding chapter that the problem of choosing a profession arises during adolescence and at this stage one is not in a position to take a correct decision. In order to help him during this crisis, it is necessary for parents to have a correct knowledge of his aptitude. We have already discussed the adolescent's personal interests in the preceding chapter and shall now deal with his social interests. A study of his social interest is very necessary for his correct guidance. In the present age of science a man has ample spare time and the problem of unemployment is also mounting every day. Social interests are particularly related to spare time because their expression takes place when an individual has some spare time. Proper guidance for the adolescent is necessary so that he may make good use of his spare time.

Interests Depends on Four Factors

With age the interests of an individual undergo changes. The interests of a child differ from those of an adolescent and those of the adolescent differ from those of an adult. The interests of the adolescent are mostly related to his future life and their development is based on four factors. These factors are sex, intelligence, environment and opportunity. As far as sex is concerned, the interests of a boy differ from those of the girls. Similarly the interests of an adolescent possessing sharp intelligence differ from those of a dull one. The environment is also responsible for difference in interests of two adolescents. An individual's development is conditioned by the opportunities he gets in his life. On getting an opportunity an adolescent may become a doctor or an engineer or any thing else. Thus interests are closely linked with sex, intelligence, environment and opportunity.

Development of Interests Useful in Life

An individual's interests are to a large extent for making his life happy or unhappy. If he gets an opportunity to act according to his interest he feels happy otherwise he leads an unhappy and frustrated life. This may be substantiated by the optionals that a student chooses for himself. If he studies subject of his liking he is satisfied. If he is made to study a subject against his liking, he feels unhappy. An individual should, therefore, be asked to do work of his liking. However, in practical life it is not always possible. An individual has to create interest in himself for the works necessary in life. Adolescence is a period of preparations for facing the realities of future life and, therefore, it will be in the interest of the adolescent to develop as many good interests in life as possible.

Development of Social Interests

It is very important to take into consideration the aptitude of an individual in developing his interests because it is then easy to develop them. For instance, if an individual does not have an aptitude for medical profession, it will be difficult to create in him an interest for it. It is also worth keeping in mind that it is not good to develop interest in an unplanned manner. Interests should be such as may be useful in social life. An individual has to develop social interests in life whether he has the ability or not because these are very necessary for leading a good social life, because an individual cannot live away from the society. An adolescent does not have too much experience of social life and, therefore, cannot take correct decision relating to social interests. The responsibility, therefore, falls on parents and teachers for providing a psychological atmosphere for developing social interests. The social interests of an individual will be in his interest and also in the interest of the society, because the welfare of society cannot be separated from that of the individual.

Instability of Adolescent's Interests

An adolescent is mostly very enthusiastic about his interests and sometimes goes beyond his limits. He is ready to go to any extent in fulfilling his interests, but he also introduces changes in his interests in no time. Gradually, with advancement in age he appears to be inclined towards stability. This stabilising process also affects his interests. Stability in interests is governed by ones environment.

Social interests of an adolescent mean those interest of an individual on the basis of which he comes in contact with his friends or the society at large. Now we come to these interests.

A Strong Desire for Gossipping

Adolescent have a strong desire to enter into conversation with others. The girls particularly show a strong tendency towards this. Even those who appear shy and dull during childhood show keen desire to talk when they get an opportunity. The reason is perhaps that during adolescence an individual is very keen to establish his personality and for this purpose he resorts to conversation thinking it to be the best medium for achieving his cherished desire. If he is unable to personally talk face to face with his friends he writes letters to them. If he finds difficulty in entering into correspondence, he then on some pretext goes to his friend's house. He wants to spend much of his time in conversation with his friends. The adolescent's friends enter into conversation the moment they gather at a meeting-ground. They also talk too much with each other in the class-room and elsewhere. In class-room when scolded by teachers, they become quiet but in meetings they will not keep quiet despite repeated warnings. They also talk in whispers in order to avoid disturbing others. This habit is common both in boys and girls. They even do not stop talking during drama, circus or a show. It is very necessary to give expression to inner feelings through conversation. So it will be unpsychological to stop them from talking with others whenever they can.

The adolescent mostly likes talking himself rather than listening to others. In a friendly company each boy wants to speak, and it is difficult for him to remain silent and listen to others. It is generally seen that in a school a meeting of adolescents is started in an orderly manner but soon it becomes disorderly because each one tries to speak.

However, during a meeting some adolescents appear very quiet. This is because they suffer from inferiority complex and not that they do not want to speak. They also have a desire to give expression to their feelings in a meeting. In fact, their desire gets suppressed within their own heart. They feel frustrated but such adults indulge into day-dreams very often and imagine as if they were taking part in the meeting. Some adolescents express their feelings through writing instead of through conversation. But such adolescents are not large in number.

KINDS OF GOSSIPS

The gossips of adolescents may be of many types depending upon his mental development and environment. The adolescent learns the art of conversation gradually. In the beginning his conversation appears childish. He may say anything before others without thinking. Gradually, he realises his shortcomings. The conversation of adolescents may be divided into three categories — gossip, discussion and reasoning. Now we shall understand each one of these below:

Gossip

In this chapter by gossip we mean such a conversation which has no pre-determined plan and which simply aims at entertainment and killing time. When some boys of different social environments and with intimate friendship assemble at a place, they then indulge into a type of conversation which may be called gossip. In gossips no personal problem is discussed, nor are these gossips motivated by any desire to solve any problem. The subjects of such gossips cover a wide range. They may relate to insignificant happenings or sports or subjects related to international happenings. The talk is conducted in a very light manner and it does not take much time from switching from one subject to another. Personal things may also figure occasionally in gossips, but of course they do not aim at solving a problem. Some boys also indulge in undesirable acts during gossip. During such acts of Holliganism, the boys may also cross the bounds of social decency and indulge in irrelevant talks. By seeing such scenes people think that these boys do not come from healthy environment. However, after some time the boys themselves start realising that their such acts are worth condemning and are stigmas on good characters. Gradually the boys mend themselves.

Discussion

A discussion may be superior to gossip. Children select a topic and discuss among themselves its good and bad points. Such a discussion may be planned and intimate friends may also be informed or requested to participate. Many children find discussions more satisfying because through them they get an opportunity to express their ideas in a disciplined manner.

Reasoning

Reasoning is on a higher footing than discussion. While reasoning everyone expresses his view one by one. Sometimes unpleasantness is created during heat of reasoning. The girls even go to the extent of abusing each other. Reasoning is an art, so it has to be learnt. In the early adolescence the boys or girls do not know how to reason but by middle adolescence they learn it.

Importance of Conversation

All these type of conversations are very important for the adolescents although some adults consider them a sheer waste of time and energy on the part of adolescents. However, it is not correct to say that by indulging in such conversations the adolescents show indifference towards their duty and responsibility. Different type of conversations generate different ideas and consequently their knowledge improves. They get acquainted with other people's views through conversations. This makes their outlook wider and more liberal. They also learn the art of eloquence through conversation.

GROUP FUNCTIONS

Strong Desire to Participate

A young child likes to take part in group functions because he expects some good refreshment there. Besides, he gets an opportunity to wear good clothes at the time. This desire is also present in an adolescent. Therefore, he is keen to attend a function whether social or otherwise.

Desire for Freedom

The girls are particularly more enthusiastic in attending such functions because they get an opportunity on such occasions to put on good clothes and go out. It is very important for them because in our social structure girls get very few opportunities for outing. In these functions boys want that participants should be mostly of their age, because then they can express themselves freely. On such occasions they do not like the presence of elders, because they feel shy before them in doing things as they wish. They do not enjoy at all elders' company at such functions and feel bored if they are to remain for long in their company. The boys even do not like to go to such functions. The fact is that adolescents want to organise functions according to their free will. They always want to arrange refreshment during the function and do not like to take the consent of elders for this purpose. They also want to provide enough edibles during the functions so that everyone may get things sufficiently. They feel disappointed if items served at the tables are not enough. They feel hurt if guardians interfere in any way in functions organised by them. Evidently, they want complete freedom in functions they organise.

TENDENCY TO CRITICISE

During Middle Adolescence

The adolescent gets more experienced and wise by the middle adolescence and understands better the good or bad points of his environment. He also feels encouraged in criticising others and occasionally gives his opinion about a problem or about the goodness or worthlessness of an issue. He also puts forward suggestions for effecting improvements. Leal[1] in his studies has observed that a desire for giving suggestions for improvement is not present in an individual during early adolescence but by the time he enters middle adolescence he develops this trait. The tendency of criticising others depends on the environment. The boys who live under strict control have a weaker inclination for criticising others. However, an adolescent now and then gets irritated and develops a desire of criticising the members of the family.

Fearless in Criticising

An individual during middle adolescence may show fearlessness in criticising others. He even may criticise the teaching method of the teacher in class and put forward suggestions to effect improvement. He fears less in criticising his classmates. He may directly criticise his friends for their styles of walking, dressing and speaking.

Criticism of Parents

After the middle adolescence the individual even begins to find faults with his parents and other elders. Earlier he used to regard them as his ideal but now he finds shortcomings in them. But he does not find himself in a position to say anything openly. The reason behind this silence is that he still expects help from them and considers himself safe and secure under them. But this does not mean that he closes his eyes towards their shortcomings. At times he criticises them and it is also possible that he may quarrel with them. All adolescents want their parents to be liberal, honest, just and helpful to others. They do not want their parents to be quarrelsome. They expect self-control in them. The adolescents look down with contempt upon corporal punishments inflicted on them by their parents. It is not necessary that adolescents may criticise their parents on their face. They often criticise them before their friends. Thus they find solace by giving vent to their feelings.

Criticism of Household Affairs

The adolescent does not hesitate in criticising the household affairs if he finds them against his aesthetic taste. He wants to decorate his house according to his taste. The rural adolescent tells where cattle should be kept and what arrangements should be made to feed them.

If the existing arrangements are not to his liking he will try to arrange them according to his choice. He himself wants to fix up pictures in rooms. Similarly, the urban adolescent wants to give suggestions in house keeping. The girls are more eager in this respect as compared to boys. They do not remain inactive after giving a suggestion but also start acting accordingly. They do not care if their mother does not approve their suggestions and actions.

Criticism of the School

In the school-going adolescents a tendency is seen these days to flout the orders of the principal and criticise him or her openly. If some action is taken against them, they will not hesitate in declaring a strike. They will not hesitate in expressing their resentment against the principal's interference in games, rustication of a student or disciplinary action against a teacher. Besides they also try to dictate terms in the process of effecting a compromise. If the principal does not act according to their desire they will try to give more aggressive colour to their protest. They also instigate their guardians to raise their voice against the principal. They may also declare a strike call to all the educational institutions in the area. If they do not resort to strike, they indulge in strong criticism and so arrange it that it reaches the ears of the principal and other teachers.

TENDENCY TO HELP OTHERS

It is commonly observed that adolescent cannot remain indifferent towards the affairs of others unlike adults. They are much concerned with others' comforts and troubles. They are easily moved seeing others in distress. They also try to motivate their parents towards helping others and on not getting satisfactory response they even take to arguing with their parents. The tendency to help others is very necessary for the mental and moral development of the adolescent. This develops the twin virtues of self-confidence and self-respect in the adolescents. Consequently, they derive immense pleasure from it. The adolescents who pass a tensed life and do not get an opportunity to express their natural feelings, they think more for helping others, because by so doing they get self-confidence and satisfaction.

Opportunity Necessary

When the adolescent develops confidence in his abilities and feels that he can stand on his own legs, the tendency of helping others gradually disappears from him and he becomes self-centred. In helping others the adolescent considers his advice and service as his main instruments. Sometimes he extends some advice without being called for. He often has to face snubbing from elders for giving uncalled for advice. He considers those persons as fools who do not follow his advice. In addition to giving uncalled advice to others, an adolescent also wants to participate in local social activities. Sometimes the desire to render social service becomes so strong that he wants to make it the aim of his life. Choosing of careers like medical practice, nursing or teaching is perhaps motivated by this desire of social service. Thus it will be good to give opportunities of social service to adolescents.

INTEREST IN NATIONAL AND INTERNATIONAL PROBLEMS

Interests on the Increase

Gradually, the interests of an adolescent develop. His interests are no more limited to the family or the neighbourhood, but they include national and international subjects also. He gets hurt on the deplorable condition of poor persons and injustice and exploitation they suffer. Hence he is easily influenced by forceful writers and leaders. He is liable to be mislead under the influence of emotions at this stage.

In the beginning the adolescent is either very aggressive or very conservative in his views. But he changes after getting some experience. In this change-over he sometimes faces frustrations and disappointments. In the end he takes to the middle course and gives up the tendency to act under impulsive conditions.

SUMMARY

Adolescence is a stage of revolution in an individual's life. So the parents and other elders should deal with him in a psychological manner.

With growth in age the interests of adolescents also undergo a change. The development of interests is influenced by sex, intelligence, environment and opportunity. Much of the success and happiness of an individual depends on opportunities available.

Interests during early adolescence are instable in nature, but gradually they become stable and by the end of adolescence the interest get more or less confirmed. However, the environment also plays an important part in stabilising interests.

Conversation is very necessary for the healthy mental and social development of an individual. The conversation may be divided into three categories—gossip, discussion and reasoning. Gossip is unplanned. Discussion is of a higher order than conversation. Reasoning may be placed in the highest category. Gossip, discussion and reasoning are related to early, middle and late adolescence respectively, because the art of conversation develops gradually.

Adolescents are very keen in organising group functions because they get an opportunity to express themselves thereby. However, they do not like the company of elders on such occasions because they feel that they cannot enjoy full freedom in their presence.

During the middle adolescence the individual develops a tendency of criticising others and by grows fearless in this process. He even does not refrain from criticising his teachers, parents, and other elders, if they behave against his desire.

During adolescence the individual appears very helpful in nature. Gradually, he develops confidence in himself and becomes self-centred. He also starts taking interest in national and international affairs.

Exercises

1. Discuss the nature of social interests during adolescence.
2. Distinguish between gossip, discussion and reasoning as modes of conversation during adolescence.
3. Discuss the necessity of guidance during adolescence.
4. Discuss the tendency of criticising others during adolescence.

Notes

1. Leal, M.A., *Physiological Maturity in Relation to Certain Characteristics of Boys and Girls,* Philadelphia; University of Pennsylvania, 1929.

7

Recreational Interests

Sources of Adolescents' Recreation

The main source of recreation during adolescence is play and it takes various forms. For recreation an individual resorts to play throughout his life, but with the development of age the form of play changes. During childhood play is purely a play with no strings attached to it but an adolescent's play is not confined to recreation alone. It may also become a matter of prestige and a competitive spirit may pervade in a play and each participant may not be at the top. Everyone tries to snatch some time from his main job for recreation. According to Wrenn Harley[1] for adults there can be four sources of recreation. They are :

(1) Opportunity to participate in games and sports,
(2) Opportunity for getting constructive experience,
(3) Opportunity to participate in social life, and
(4) Provision of sources of recreation in the home.

Sources of Recreation Depend on Environment

We know that all adolescents do not get equal opportunities. In fact, their availability depends largely on environment. In our Indian social structure the girls get fewer opportunities in comparison to boys. Similarly, adolescents from the poorer section of the society get comparatively fewer opportunities. The proper physical, mental, social, moral and religious development of an adolescent depends to a great extent on various type of opportunities. It is, therefore, the duty of the parents to provide these opportunities as far as possible.

Change in Recreational Interests

As an individual grows, his recreational interests undergo changes. For example a young baby may play with small toys, a more grown up baby will like to play with moving toys, a six-year old child will prefer to play with other children and more grown up children will like to play with other things. In the child's play physical labour is largely involved but in adolescents there is a decline of the element of physical labour. An adolescent is prone to get recreation from such things as playing-cards, chess, cinema, radio, and novels etc. Many adolescents also are inclined to play hockey, foot-ball or cricket but because these games entail money and too much of physical labour, therefore, most of the adolescents are unable to resort to such kinds of recreation. The recreational interests change very slowly and it may be said that it is related to physical development. As the physical development is a slow moving process, so is the recreational interest.

Lack of Sources for Recreation

Smaller children have plenty of time to play, but this is not the case with adolescents whose social responsibilities increase with increase in age. If an adolescent comes from a poor family, he is worried for money. He, therefore, takes to that type of recreation which neither claims much money nor much time. The scope of recreation, therefore, gets limited in the case of adolescents. The other reasons are that the adolescent loses interest in childish plays. Secondly, his interests appear to be similar to those of adults and he has to devote energy to many other activities. So he is short of time also. He is also worried sometimes in his family affairs. The scope of recreation may be narrowed down due to unfavourable circumstances.

SOME POPULAR TYPE OF RECREATIONS OF ADOLESCENTS

Difference in Methods of Recreation according to Mental Development

It is difficult to name any particular recreation which may be equally popular amongst all. This is because no two individuals possess the same nature. Hence with the difference in nature the liking for recreation also differs. Naturally it is difficult to name any such recreation which may be equally popular. However, some such forms of recreations may be mentioned which are generally popular among adolescents. Adolescents want to observe some pre-fixed rules in their games. Children, adolescents and adults see films, dramas and other plays, but a difference may be seen in their way of seeing, listening and reading objects. This difference depends upon individual's mental development.

Adolescent's Games have more Social Touch

There is a greater social touch in the games of adolescents who prefer to play in groups or teams. This is also due to the growth of competitive spirit in them. Keeping this aspect in view one may call the team games like football, hockey, cricket etc., as social games.

During childhood individuality in games is more prominent, because the desire of self-expression is very strong in children. Therefore, it is difficult for the child to sacrifice his individuality in the interest of team spirit. This tendency gradually vanishes and when he reaches adolescence, he is ready to give up his individuality for team spirit or for the development of his group or organisation. During adolescence an individual takes some pride in the name of his party and its fame, but during childhood he may take pride in his individual performance.

Difference in the Games of Young Children and Adolescents

Adolescents' games are organised and pre-planned as compared to children's games. In case of children as soon as two or three of them gather at a place they begin to play some game without any pre-determined plan of place or game, whereas adolescents decide the team, place, game and rules etc., before starting or participating in a game. They also decide the uniform to wear in a particular game. The children's on the other hand, start playing without caring about dress, place or game. They may play anywhere and at any place and without going into the merit of their playing tools. Poor boys design their own playing tools. They will prepare football from old clothes or hockeys from ordinary stick or pieces of fire wood. But the adolescent would not do so. He will insist on proper dress and good implements for a game. In fact, the adolescents' approach to games is somewhat artificial while those of children is natural to a greater extent. Their mode of play is also artificial because of being influenced by the environment. These changes often prove hurdles for many poor adolescents who cannot afford to purchase costly equipments like tennis, rackets or balls or flannels and blazers for the game of cricket.

Use of Intelligence by Adolescents in Games

Adolescents use their intelligence while playing, whereas in the children's game it is the chance that plays a more prominent part. The use of intelligence may be seen when an adolescent plays cards, chess or solve puzzles. It takes them hours to complete a game and they get so absorbed in the play that they even forget food and work. They also resort to gambling for recreation and praise their intelligence if they win and blame their fortune, if they lose. Environment is largely responsible for unhealthy recreations. So adolescents should be saved from bad environment.

Games of Adolescent Girls

There is a marked difference between the games played by adolescent girls and boys because by nature the girls do not prefer to play such games which involve physical labour, although sometimes they do play games like hockey and football. The girls from well-to-do families manage to play costly games like tennis and badminton involving physical labour. But in our country the number of such girls is negligible. In fact, our society is such that many girls never get an opportunity to play outdoor games. They mostly pass their time in household affairs after coming from schools and colleges. It is difficult to determine the scope of such girls' games and sports. Their main recreation is cutting jokes or indulging into gossips with girls of their own age. Even this is resented by many parents.

COLLECTING ARTICLES

According to Mental Development

Some adolescents develop the hobby of collecting costly articles and this serve as a recreation for them. This tendency of collecting article is also present in children but the articles of collection vary in quality and quantity according to the mental development of the individual. A collection of a young child may contain nothing more than broken glasses, pencils, pictures and books on cats and dogs. But a more grown up child's collection may contain other things. Similarly an adolescent's collection may contain still better articles, of course, depending on his environment and financial condition. According to Witty and Lehman[2] there is a strong desire to collect articles in boys and girst between the age of 9 to 13 years and generally the collection of such boys and girls contain 8 to 10 articles. By the age of 14 this desire starts disappearing because adolescents of 15 or 16 years of age are seen collecting only 4 to 6 articles and those aged 17 or 18 only collecting three or four articles. Sullenger[3] found during his studies that in High School only 18 per cent girls and 10 per cent boys were engaged in collection of articles.

Difference in Interests in Articles according to Environment

The interest of individuals differ according to the environment in which they grow up. A boy brought up in an urban environment has different interest from that of one brought up in a rural environment. Similarly, the environment which pervades in the home also influences one's interests. For instance, a rural boy will be attracted towards cups and plates, while the urban boy will show interest in earthen jars. A rural boy will not care to drink sugarcane juice, while the urban boy will relish it. According to Witty and Lehman rural boys comparatively mature late than urban boys. So the desire to collect articles continue longer in them.

Difference between the Collections of Boys and Girls

The main difference between the collecting hobbies of boys and girls according to Whitley[4] is that while girls collect more in quantity and the boys go for wider variety. Witty and Lehman are of the opinion that girls are more fond of collecting things appealing to aesthetic sense and relating to cosmetics, while boys are more interested in collecting insects and different limbs of small harmless animals.

Purpose of Collecting Things

Behind the collection of articles there are various purposes although in young children often the collection is aimless or senseless and is merely for a fun. Older children collect with the purpose of self-expression or by motivated by some need. However, there are some adolescents who collect things out of sheer craze.

TENDENCY TO DISCOVER

Its Characteristic and Difficulties of Adolescents in our Country

A tendency to make new discoveries is present both in the child and the adolescent, although the scope of activity is limited in the case of children because they are either afraid of going too far away from their homes or are not allowed by their guardians to stay away from the home. This is not the case with adolescents and they have greater freedom in this respect. He is also not much afraid in going and staying away from the home. He is even keen to go to strange places and find out new things there. The adolescents also desire to travel by ships and planes and visit foreign lands. It is very difficult for the adolescents to fulfil their desires. They, therefore, keep themselves satisfied by reading books on foreign countries or by day-dreaming or doing some other things.

Out of Parent's Control

There is a desire in an adolescent to be free and when he is fed up with the control exercised by parents, he rebels and wants to satisfy his desires independently. He wants to go out and walk, talk, eat and enjoy according to his free will. He thinks his parents to be obstacles in the path of satisfying his desires. Although the adolescent wants to satisfy his curiosities independently, yet he desires friends, company. He is not much inclined to go away alone.

Constructing Articles for the Sake of Pleasure

The desire of doing some constructive work is present in every one upto some extent and this desire is very strong in younger children. They make small houses out of clay or prepare garlands from flowers. All these indicate the presence of constructive tendency. The child gets immense pleasure in constructing some thing. Similarly, adolescents also get pleasure by making something. Creating new things is a source of recreation to the adolescents. Adults while creating an article are motivated by monetary gains, but this is not the case with adolescents. The adolescent derives pleasure like the young children but there is always a suspicion in his mind that others may make fun of his creation. If he gets slightest hint of condemnation or contemptuous treatment he immediately destroys the article or remakes it. This tendency is more prominent in adolescent girls. They will immediately destroy or unmake what they had made and make a fresh beginning in an effort to get appreciation.

Effect of Environment and Development

In making articles it is the environment that plays a prominent part. Adolescents prefer the trade which is practised in the home. For example, an adolescent from a clay modeller family will make clay pots, from a blacksmith family will like to make iron instruments, from gold-smith family gold, silver, jewels and so on. Girls from educated family will like to write, from artist family will make pictures or will like sewing, weaving or tailoring clothes. Both adolescent boys and girls take keen interest in interior decoration. But with advance in age their interests in making things decline. May be the reason that the added responsibilities leave little time or criticisms and competitions discourage them.

Different Reading Tastes at Different Ages

Reading is a very important source of recreation and has two purposes namely, recreation and learning. It is true that the adolescent has no time for any one of them because his mind is more engaged in many real and imaginary problems. Some of his problems are born out of his own fancy. The truth is that they do exist. According to Terman and Lima[5] recreational reading reaches the climax at the age of 12 or 13 years. After that the aim of reading does not remain recreation. At the age of eleven a boy likes to read books describing courageous deeds and detective stories. The boys like to read books on science and inventions while girls like stories relating to house and schools. At the age of 12 boys develop interest in all kinds of stories. At this age he likes to read mythological and historical stories of brave characters. He also likes reading the lives of great men and women. They show great enthusiasm in reading them. According to Jordan[6] reading interests undergo a change at the age of 14 years. This change is clearly individualistic in character. The adolescent now likes to read one single subject. He is not inclined to read whatever comes to hand. By the age of 16 this inclination about studying a particular subject becomes quite strong and gives the appearance of a mature decision. And now from this age the purpose of reading is more of obtaining knowledge and the object of recreation gradually declines.

Boys' Interests

Because boys and girls have to face different responsibilities in future life, their reading interests naturally differ. According to Terman and Lima the interest of boys after the age of 14 years declines for reading books on courageous deeds. Now they develop a taste for reading biographies and about travels, sports and scientific inventions. At the age of 15 years they start concentrating on one single subject. At 16 they want to read about international happenings and other books pertaining to some knowledge. After that age their reading interests appear to become like those of adults.

Girls' Interests

During the early childhood girls, like boys, love to read fairy tales. They are at this age away from realities and roam in an imaginary world, but this tendency changes during adolescence. They now develop taste for reading literature full of tense emotional feelings. They very much like books involving suspense. They very seriously read books relating to school life or historical novel with hair-raising stories. They also like to read poems. According to Hildreth[7] the girls have more liking or show greater taste in reading mystery and detective stories, novels and love stories than boy do.

Newspapers

The adolescent gradually develops taste for reading newspapers. During early adolescence he has no taste for reading newspapers. Gradually, he develops some taste for newspapers but that does not mean that he starts taking interests in serious news or views on national or international affairs. He reads newspapers in order to know about local happenings, jokes, cheap articles, film advertisements and sports news. The adolescent girls like to read advertisements relating to cosmetics and household matters. The newspaper reading habit in

India is not common in the people as compared to those in some western countries, because the percentage of literacy is quite low. Even heads of educational institutions in India pose that they do not get enough time to read newspapers. So is the case with numerous educated heads of the family. In such an environment to expect adolescents to develop newspaper reading habit is surprising.

Magazines

We find that some adolescents have taste for reading magazines. Children like to see pictures in the magazine and do not appear to be interested in reading the content. So they turn over the pages of magazines occasionally in order to see pictures. The reasons of adolescents reading magazine is because they are comparatively cheaper and are easily available in reading rooms. The magazine also deal with topics of current importance. Therefore, the adolescent is more inclined towards magazines. Magazines are also attractive than books because they are illustrated and have chapters on varied subjects. The books for adolescents are mostly unillustrated although the children's books do contain some pictures. It is, therefore, natural that adolescents are inclined to read magazines. Adolescent boys like to read such magazines which contain interesting anecdotes, incidents, fun, political and social subjects and stories related to scientific inventions. Adolescent girls are more inclined towards magazines containing literature on film heroes and actresses, household matters and advertisements relating to beauty aids.

MUSIC

More Interest in Music Now

In India people are now taking more interest in music than before. It is no more considered a vocation of degraded families and is not looked down upon. Earlier music was not considered respectable in some rich and advanced families, but a change has come in people's thinking during the last five decades and some importance is now attached to music. However, this has to be admitted that music has yet not been given that place in colleges and schools which is being given to other subjects. Since it is now not looked down upon, therefore, adolescent boys and girls are attracted towards it. Every human being knows to laugh, weep or sing by nature and every one has his own style, but there is a difference between singing and music. It is not in the scope of this book to dwell upon at length about this difference. However, this much may be said that if a song is sung according to the rules and regulations provided in academic books (*Shastras*), it will be considered as a part of music. Singing, dancing and playing of musical instrument form three important aspects of music. We shall, therefore, deal below briefly the interests of adolescents in all these three aspects.

Adolescents' Love of Music

A child loves music and likes singing, dancing and playing on some musical instrument. He feels greatly entertained on listening to others, song, dancing or playing musical instruments. The child is fond of rhythm and, therefore, he likes dancing more. Girls are comparatively more interested in music than boys. However, during adolescence the interest in music declines. That is why fewer students opt for music in intermediate and B.A. classes. In High School classes it is observed that girls generally opt for Sitar, Israj and vocal music. Very few girls opt for Tabala. As compared to girls, boys are less inclined towards taking music. They prefer to offer instrumental music, because they suspect that their voice may not prove equal to the task. Even then some offer vocal music. Music may be considered as a source of recreation only in case of those boys who learn classical music. Those who do not learn classical music sing film songs or recite poems of their favourite poets, but they do not practice music regularly. When in mood, they sing in the company of other friends. Those who learn classical music practise regularly in morning or evening. This also serves a recreation to them. Sometimes when they are tired or sad they resort to music for recreation.

RADIO AND TELEVISION

Radio has acquired a place as one of the main sources of recreation in the modern world. However, in a poor country like India there is a great shortage of radios and it is not found in all the homes. In rural areas radios in houses are rare and therefore it should not be considered as a main and important source of recreation in India. In urban areas, however, many houses do possess radio-sets, but they are generally not in the control of adolescents. Parents generally keep them in their supervision and the adolescent finds it difficult to tune it according to his choice. The position of adolescents in rich countries like U.S.A. and England is different where parents provide separate radio sets to their children. So it may be considered as an important source of recreation for adolescent there. In rich foreign countries television is also one of the sources of recreation. In India also, now television is becoming very popular and most of the people living in cities have their own T.V. sets. In India even many rural families own transistors which are just Radio sets. Thus Radio and T.V. have now become common sources of recreation Radio is so common in some western countries that as soon as a boy enters home he switches on his radio and enjoys it while doing work. They are so crazy about it that many of them think that they will not be able to do any work if they do not listen to radio while doing work.

Particular Interest in Radio

Adolescent boys are particularly interested in certain radio programmes. They have special liking for film song programmes, although they do not object to listening to other programmes because it entertains them. Listening to radio cricket commentary has become a craze in Indian boys. Similarly Radio Ceylon and some comic programmes are getting popularity. Radio and television are now powerful media for building the character of adolescents. These media may be gainfully used in educating them.

CINEMA

Interest according to Maturity of Mind

Cinema has a great impact on the minds of adolescents. In urban areas the number of cinema houses are increasing every year and despite increase in entertainment tax the crowd at cinema houses is ever increasing. Films are greatly influencing the character of adolescent because they go towards a cinema house the moment they have some money to spare. It is at present leading adolescents on the wrong and harmful side. The rural boys, however, are not much influenced by cinemas because they do not get many opportunities to see them. If, there, are other source of entertainment the adolescent's may not see the films so often but unfortunately other healthy entertainments are so few in India that young adolescents usually go to cinemas for entertainments. However, as the adolescent's mind matures his interest in films declines. Adolescents living in healthy environment care little for Cinema shows but they are very crazy about different types of T.V. serials. Other reasons for decline in interest towards cinema are lack of money and time and family and social pre-occupations.

Film-Interest

Although an adolescent will like to see film which is in accordance with his reading taste, but it is not necessary that he may refuse to see other films. In fact, he mostly goes to films which fall in line with his taste. There is some difference in the taste of girls and boys. Girls prefer romantic and suspense films more, while boys prefer comedies, detective or war documentaries. However, it is the actors who influence the choice considerably. Their presence in the film is enough to attract the adolescent to the Cinema house. During adolescence both boys and girls are hero-worshippers and girls are comparatively more inclined towards hero-worshipping. They, therefore, hold actors and actresses in high esteem and it is no wonder that they try to emulate them. By the end of adolescence the individual stops hero-worship and wants to satisfy his or her desire for love by getting married.

Effect of Cinemas on Adolescents

Although cinemas do not influence younger children much yet they greatly influence the adolescents in many walks of life. Cinemas leave deep impression on an adolescent's mind and bring a revolutionary change in the mental and physical attitude in them. They derive inspiration from film in dressing themselves, decorating their homes and even adopting hair styles shown in films. Their manner of conversation and walking also is influenced by films. The desire to get fame, money and love are also influenced by films.

PETS

Adolescents' Interests for Pets

Small domestic pets have great attraction. Most of the children want to have pets, preferably dogs, cats and birds. The most popular pet for boys is a dog and next comes the cat. Even calf, young ones of a goat or monkey are liked by boys. They love to touch and play with them. When they become a bit older they are attracted towards birds like parrot, coloured sparrows or beautiful peacocks or pigeons. The desire to tame birds is quite prominent in an adolescent. In rural area boys are fond of 'teetars'. Girls have a greater attraction for birds. The desire to have a pet dog continues even during adolescence. In rural areas adolescent have also a liking for taming pet animals like young ones of horses and cows. A pet animal is a great consolation for an adolescent who feels frustrated or disappointed or neglected by others. They serve as a source or channel for giving vent to their feelings. When unhappy or in dejected mood, the pets serve as a source of entertainment. However, if an adolescent is happy with his social environment he cares less for pets.

IMPORTANCE OF HEALTHY ENTERTAINMENT IN THE DEVELOPMENT OF ADOLESCENTS

Healthy entertainment plays an important role in building the character of adolescents. So it will be worthwhile to throw some light on this subject.

For building a good personality a spirit of competition is necessary. Competition indicates to the individual what he lacks and what he possesses. He gets an idea of his capabilities and his weakness. As a result he may take steps to remove his shortcomings and get ready to bear the burden of social responsibilities. During childhood the individual remains under the control of elders and, therefore, is unable to find out his shortcomings. He is also not in a position then to compare his capabilities independently with those of others. During adolescence the control of elders loosens and the adolescent gets more freedom. It is, therefore, necessary for the guardians to allow him to enjoy different types of entertainment so that he may get an opportunity to come in closer contacts with the society.

An adolescent experiences self-fulfilment from entertainment during leisure. This experience gives him some self-reliance. During adolescence the individual generally passes his leisure in idleness and he does not get an opportunity of healthy entertainment. If he gets opportunity to develop his various faculties, he will be in a better position to solve his various future problems.

Entertainment develops in an adolescent moral values. Since during entertainment, he is not under control, he tries to exercise control over himself and tries to stand on his own feet. This helps in developing moral qualities in him.

He also learns social values and learns to bear responsibilities of a citizen. He also learns how to behave with others. It also saves them from indolence and consequently keeps him away from evil influences.

Healthy entertainment has healthy influence on the adolescent's mental and physical health. Entertainment also remove emotional tension.

In the earlier three chapters an effort has been made to discuss the various interests of adolescents. Now we propose to discuss the importance of interests and sources employed in developing them.

IMPORTANCE OF INTERESTS IN ADOLESCENT'S DEVELOPMENT

From multi-interests in life a sense of satisfaction is gained which is very useful for one's mental health. The individual becomes liberal and broad minded in his outlook. Narrow mindedness is harmful for the society and this evil has to be eradicated.

It is not in the interest of an individual to be a jack of all trades but master of none. An individual should, therefore, develop only such interests which are within his power and which he can successfully cultivate. If is not good to go on cultivating different interests at a time without reaching the top of any of them. One should only develop firm interests and concentrate his entire energy in perfecting them.

MEANS OF DEVELOPING INTERESTS

In order to find out one's real interest it is necessary to have experience of many things and activities. His field of activities should be wide. The guardians should also provide such an environment which may create a desire in the adolescent to learn and take deep interest in good things.

It is necessary for developing interest in those objects or the things which are within the power and resources of the individual. However, an individual cannot develop interest in all those things which lie within his power. He may be interested in them, but he cannot fully cultivate them. The adolescent should not be compelled to study such subjects or undertake such work in which he lacks taste. He may be encouraged towards them at certain psychological moments, but it is more proper to save him from experiencing failures because failure develops in an individual a feeling of inferiority complex. This retards his progress in other fields also. Hence it is necessary to give him such a work in which he may achieve success.

The environment around the adolescent should be such as to inspire him. Self-inspiration makes the individual go ahead and this also creates in him real interests. An individual feels a sense of satisfaction when he acts according to his inspiration and this sense of self-satisfaction proves very helpful in giving a permanent footing towards some thing good. In the earlier stages one has to find out the direction in which lies the interest of the adolescent. He should, therefore, be given an opportunity to gain experience of different things. When he comes across different experiences he himself comes to know about his interests and then he can easily take to his real interests.

SUMMARY

Healthy entertainment is very necessary for the mental and physical development of an individual. Play is a very important entertainment. However, the quality of play varies according to age. An adolescent may not like to take part in those types of plays which the child will like to enjoy. Entertainment should be of four categories :

1. Opportunity to participate in games and sports,
2. Opportunity to acquire constructive experience,
3. Opportunity to lead good social life, and
4. Entertainment in the home.

The sources of entertainment depend on the environment. All adolescents do not get equal opportunities. Parents provide mediums of entertainment interests relating to entertainment undergo changes gradually and the change occures with advance in age.

In India an adolescent has less sources of entertainment as compared to those in foreign countries.

Collection of articles, efforts to discover new things, constructing things, reading, music, film shows, radio and keeping pets are some of the important forms of entertainments of adolescents. The interests of children differ from those of adolescents and among adolescents the interests differ between girls and boys. The boys prefer games and sports, reading books of courageous deeds or discoveries, while girls go for indoor games and books on romance and suspense. The boys prefer instrumental music while girls are more interested in vocal music than boys.

By the end of adolescence there is a decline in certain interests, because of social and family responsibilities and lack of time and money.

Entertainments and interests play a vital role in the development of an individual's character and personality. They also keep the adolescent pre-occupied thus keeping him away from many evil influences. Efforts should, therefore, be made to provide the adolescent with opportunities for indulging into healthy entertainments. He should also be helped to find out his real interests.

Exercises

1. What are the sources of adolescents' interests?
2. Describe the nature of recreations resorted to generally by adolescents.
3. Distinguish between games of adolescent boys and those of adolescent girls.
4. Distinguish between interests of adolescent boys and those of adolescent girls.
5. Discuss the importance of healthy entertainment and interests in the development of adolescents.

Notes

1. Wrenn, C.G. and Harley, D.L., *Time on their Hands a Report on Leisure, Recreation and Young People.* American Council on Education, Washington, 1941.
2. Witty, P.A. and Lehman, H.C. 'Further Studies of Children's Interest in Collecting', *J. Educ. Psychol.* 21, 112-127, 1930.

3. Sullenger, T.E., 'Extracurricular Leisure Time, *Activities Recreation*, 32, 509-510, 1938.
4. Whitley, M.T. 'Children's Interest in Collecting' *J. Edu. Psychol.* 20, 249-261, 1929.
5. Terman, L.M., and Lima, M.K. *Children's Reading*. Appleton-Century, New York, 1927.
6. Jordan, A.M., *Children's Interest in Reading*, Chappel Hill N.C.
7. Hildreth, G., 'Adolescent Interests and Abilities', *J. Gennet Psychol.* 43, 65-93, 1933.

8

Friendship and Leadership during Adolescence

Friendship during Adolescence

Making friendship with others is a natural desire of a human being whether he is young or old. Children try to befriend other children, but their friendship hangs on a weak thread. Under emotional impact they make friends and also break the friendship in no time. But in the case of adolescents the bonds of friendship are stronger. They try to make their friendship permanent. They even make great sacrifices in maintaining friendship. The adolescents make friendship on the basis of qualities and not on nearness of homes. A neighbour may not be an adolescent's friend, while one living at a long distance may become his fast friend. We shall now understand the nature of friendship during adolescence :

Cautious Approach in Selecting Friends

An adolescent is very cautious and independent in choosing his friends. He will not enter into friendship with others on the recommendation of any one else. He may associate with others but that does not mean that he has established friendship with them. He will not even choose his friends on the advice of his parents. He may however, become ready to break friendship with others if his parents oppose the friendship. During adolescence one is not experienced enough to judge an individual's character and, therefore, he may select wrong friends. He soon quarrels with persons wrongly chosen as friends. This is more frequently the case with emotional boys. It is commonly seen that friendship made under the influence of emotion does not last long. An adolescent realises that it is not proper to enter into bonds of friendship on the basis of physical appearance or impressive conversation. So he adopts a cautious approach according to his common sense in making friendship. The change in friendship does not happen frequently by the time the adolescence phase is over. By this time the individual succeeds in making friendship with good persons and such friendship lasts for a long time.

Emphasis on the Selection of Good Friends

During early adolescence an individual mostly makes friendship with persons of similar tastes. Age is also a consideration in choosing friends. An adolescent does not like too much of disparity in age between himself and his friends. An adolescent is inclined to make friendship with those from whom he can get help in solving some of his problems. In the beginning an adolescent wants to make a large number of friends because he thinks that he can command respect only when he has a wide friend circle. Most of the boys and girls during early adolescence try to make a number of friends and in this respect their taste appears to be similar. However, by the time one reaches middle adolescence this tendency of making numerous friend declines and one now attaches greater importance to choosing good friends. Adolescents now think that in good company they will develop good qualities and thus be able to command respect from others. The other reason for making fewer friends is that at this time they do not have enough leisure and whatever leisure time they have, they want to spend it in company of such friends who may be useful. For example, a studious boy will like to make another studious boy his friend or a good player will similarly prefer the company of another good player.

Friendship Co-related with Socio-economic Status

Financial and social positions also count much in cultivating friendship. Those who come from the same social and financial status prefer each other's friendship. Thus it may be said that an adolescent having a rich father will try to enter into friendship with another adolescent who also comes from a wealthy family. Similarly, social status is also a consideration. Similarity in intelligence is also sometimes a consideration. It is generally seen that an intelligent boy will make friendship with an equally intelligent boy. A rich boy will hesitate to make friendship with a poor boy.

Quarrel and Jealousy among Friends

Both adolescent boys and girls do not hesitate in criticising others when an opportunity is available. This sometimes creates a rift among them and leads to quarrels. Criticisms are taken lightly by some adolescents but many take a serious view and also think of giving up friendship of the critic. The adolescent boys and girls entertain a feeling of jealousy against their friends. They ardently wish to be equal to their friends in good qualities.

LEADERSHIP DURING ADOLESCENCE

There is a natural desire of an adolescent to get the position of a leader of his friends. However, leadership calls for a number of qualities. The ability to attract and impress others, good personality, robustness, art of conversation and ability to force his views, sacrifice for others, doing social work, high ideals, determination, courage, definite programme and popularity are some of the qualities needed for leadership. Leadership is also related to circumstances. Some may successfully lead others in one particular situation, while others in a different situation. For example, a leader in wartime may not be a successful leader in peace. The case of Churchill is a glaring example of leadership. He was an excellent leader during the Second World War, but during the peace time he could not lead his country and had to lose his Prime-ministership. Evidently, different qualities are needed for leadership at different times and situations.

The Adolescent Leader and Categories of his Followers

We have explained above that an individual may be a successful leader in a particular situation, but he may prove a failure in other situations. During adolescence individuals take part in different activities according to their likings. According to Spaulding[1] adolescent leaders fall in five categories :

(1) Social leaders — Those who can lead in social activities.
(2) Intellectual leaders — Those who can lead in intellectual pursuits like delivering speeches, writing articles or reciting poems or songs.
(3) School leader — Those who take part in school activities.

(4) Sports leader — Those who are good at sports and games.
(5) All Sound leaders — Those who are brilliant in all activities.

Besides, there are leaders who are respected as leaders either due to affection or fear. Those who are followed due to affection possess the qualities of organisation, power, courage or bravery etc. Leadership due to fear may be on account of weakness of the followers or due to the fear of being harmed. Such followers have been placed in four categories by Pigors[2].

(1) Those adolescents who are not afraid of shouldering any responsibility and get busy in constructive activities at the instance of the leader. They are ambitious and have a desire to free themselves from conservatism.
(2) Those who have no initiative in themselves but obey the instructions of leaders readily and faithfully.
(3) Those who obey their leader under some emotional impact. Such followers are influenced by the personality of the leader and because of this influence they follow the leader unhesitatingly. They are even ready for self-sacrifice.
(4) Those adolescents who follow the leader due to some personal interest.

Leadership More Stable during Adolescence

Adolescent leaders are very active in social activities and may be seen participating in games and sports or some other cultural or social programmes. Those adolescents who lack the qualities of leadership devote themselves more to studies and prefer to remain aloof. During childhood, a child may lead other children but his leadership may be very instable. Some children lead others for a week or utmost for a month or two. After this another child may take his place. But this is not so during adolescence. The leadership during adolescence is comparatively more stable because it is based on certain qualities. A girl or a boy who is accepted as a leader continues to be so for a considerable time. His or her prestige and power lasts longer because his or her selection is made after considerable deliberation.

NECESSARY QUALITIES FOR LEADERSHIP

Attractive Personality

In order to establish his leadership on a permanent footing an adolescent has to be attractive. He or she has to put on good clothes and appear neat and clean before others. An adolescent indifferent towards his or her physical appearance finds it difficult to maintain his or her leadership. All this does not mean that he or she should wear costly garments and live with pomp and show. However, his or her physical appearance should not be repulsive.

Sharp Intelligence

Intelligence plays a prominent part in establishing leadership. A leader must be superior in intelligence to his followers. A leader is bound to lose his leadership if he is not superior to others in intelligence. It is on the strength of superiority of intelligence that he takes a decision and others obey him. Experiments conducted by Termann, Fleming, Moore and Reynaulds have proved that an adolescent leader is comparatively of superior intelligence to others.

Social Position

Respectable family is another asset for a leader. Studies conducted by Reynaulds, Belingrath, Ramlin and Sward reveal that adolescent leaders hail from respectable families. It is necessary to belong to a respectable family in order to influence others. It is extremely difficult for an adolescent to become a leader without having a respectable family background. It is generally seen that an individual coming from a good family inherits certain qualities which are necessary for a leader. Good family background influences the character, behaviour and physical appearance. Thus an individual's social background is intimately related to his qualities of leadership.

Good Educational Achievements

An adolescent who is good at studies is generally selected for leadership, because the teachers and others have good opinion about him. Garrison, Chapin, Sward, Jordan and Hunter also subscribe to this view. A leader should be exemplary in many respects. It is, therefore, natural that those who distinguish themselves are selected leaders.

Age

Generally, seniority in age is also a deciding factor in the selection of leaders. Adolescents do not select one as their leader if he is too junior in age. Maturity in behaviour, character and experience is related to age. Therefore, leaders are such persons who are senior in age. Moore, Browne, Remlin and Renaulds also agree with this view.

Personality

Adolescents with good and impressive personality are generally chosen as leaders. Other contributing factors are self-confidence, courage, ability to take prompt decision, originality, broad-mindedness, organisational power, good health, initiative and dash, thinking power and sympathetic attitude etc. An adolescent possessing these qualities is considered to possess a good personality. The one who abounds in these qualities during adolescence is mostly selected as a leader.

CAUSES OF SUCCESS AND FAILURE OF FRIENDSHIP

Causes of Failures

Everyone desires to command respect in the society and those who do not get respect naturally become unhappy. This desire is present in children as well as in adolescents. The adolescent who is not respected by others of his age or who is criticised by his companions remains gloomy. This state of mind also adversely affects his personality. Such adolescents then start seeking the company of either smaller children or elders or remain busy with his books or other activities as far as possible. They, therefore, are unable to acquire social qualities due to their aloofness. Such adolescents never succeed in creating friends easily. The causes for this failure may be as under :

(1) *Some kind of physical deformity* — Lame, paralysis of any limb one-eyed or deaf. Due to these shortcomings his personality is not attractive and other boys do not want to

maintain intimate social relationship with him.

(2) *Poor Social and Economic Condition* — This reason is quite clear and needs no further explanation.

(3) *Selfishness* — Too much selfishness is a disqualification, because then one will look to his own personal interest only at the cost of others.

(4) *Jealousy* — Those adolescents who are dominated by this evil fail to make friends. No adolescent will ever like to make friends with such an individual who is jealous of him.

(5) *Geographic distance* — Distance makes it difficult for friendship to grow because contact becomes difficult.

(6) *Quarrelsomeness* — Nobody will like to make friendship with a quarrelsome person.

(7) *Contrasting qualities* — People of contrasting qualities are not made friends.

(8) *Dull* — No one likes to make friendship will dullards.

(9) *Too much humility* — Such persons are considered cowards or frauds and therefore adolescents do not like him.

(10) *Too much superior* — Friendship is generally between equals and no adolescent likes to act as second fiddle. He, therefore, does not want to make friendship with an extra-ordinary brilliant adolescent for fear of being dominated all the time.

(11) *Too much air* — Those who consider themselves too high in society also fail to make friendship with others. Other adolescents consider him proudy and, therefore, do not make friendship with him.

Causes for Success

The qualities which make a child lovable may prove otherwise during adolescence. Therefore, it is possible that an individual who was loved as a child may not be liked by others when he becomes an adolescent, because the needs of childhood and adolescence are not the same. The following qualities in adolescents are appreciated by others and with their help an adolescent may succeed in making friends :

(1) Good health and attractive personality. Such adolescents are generally loved by others.

(2) Good social and economic position.

(3) Superior performance in games and other activities.

(4) Interest and sympathy with others.
(5) Different social experiences. Such adolescents leave the impact of their personality on others and do not get nervous in difficult situations.
(6) Good host—Those adolescents who are good hosts and liberally entertain friends.
(7) Good intelligence—So that he can take a decision immediately in difficult situations.
(8) Good knowledge of social activities.
(9) Discharge of responsibility faithfully.
(10) Self-control—One who does not easily loses balance of mind and gets angry.
(11) Co-operative and helpful.
(12) Unselfish.
(13) Ever ready to faithfully discharge the responsibilities of leadership.

Parent's Duty in Relation to Friendships of Adolescents

In the adolescent's mind there are too many curiosities and problems relating to life. So his emotional life is somewhat disbalanced. There can be many other factors for mental disbalance. Under such circumstances friendship has an important place in an adolescent's life and it is the responsibility of parents to adopt a very psychological approach towards their ward's friendship. The parents are also sometimes very much worried about this affair because some adolescents do not get friends and some make friendship with undesirable adolescents. This creates natural apprehensions in the minds of parents. Friendship is not only importance during adolescence but is also of great importance in adult's life. The friendship cultivated during adolescence may also last even when the friends develop into adults. An adolescent has also to learn the art of cultivating friendship and this art may also prove very helpful in future life.

Adolescents prefer to cultivate friendship with those belonging to their sex and age group, but they also consider it necessary for their future life to make friends with grown up persons and also with those belonging to opposite sex. This desire of adolescents is not easily fulfilled and sometimes they make friendship with unsuitable persons. Such persons may be termed as 'companions'. Many adults fail to understand the nature of adolescents' friendship. It is the responsibility of parents to guide their wards in this matter by showing directly or indirectly as to how to maintain friendship, and to explain the points of friendship and the different kind of behaviour that are needed with different kind of friends. The adolescent must learn the proper behaviour to be extended to the people coming in close contact on different occasions. Courtesy is the most important lesson which the adolescent must invariably learn to extend. They should not get hurt or entertain apprehensions about others behaviour in haste and without coolly deliberating over it. Strong and bitter words, discourteous replies and unconditional claim for a right are the enemies of friendship. Parents should impress upon their children to extend courteous behaviour to others but not to expect too much from acquaintances and friends otherwise they will face disappointment. The stability of friendship depends on finer qualities of one's personality. Other things like good economic condition or high social position, good physical appearance or commonness of religious or national background are of secondary importance. Some adolescents and parents lose sight of this important factor. Some adolescents overlook the qualities of personality and make friendship on the basis of secondary qualities. Such adolescents later on face disappointment. Thus in selection of friends emphasis must be laid on finer points of personality, because it helps the development of social qualities. The parents, therefore, should adopt a psychological approach.

Friendship demands fulfilling of some duties and discharge of some obligations. Only then friendship may last. In need friends expect help and sympathy from other friends. However, if the help needed smacks of anti-social activities, then it may be overlooked. For instance, if an adolescent quarrels with someone and appeals to his friends to murder him or inflict serious injuries, then such a help on the parts of the friends will be condemnable. However, friendship demands sacrifice and in the absence of sacrifice friendship cannot be maintained. It is a well known proverb that 'a friend in need is a friend indeed'. In friendship an individual has to sacrifice his own interest and help the friend. Parents must teach their children the importance of scuh a sacrifice, otherwise they will not be able to discharge their obligations towards their friends and will fall short of real friends.

It is commonly seen that friendship between two adolescents is short-lived, because one always asserts his superiority over the other, and the less dominating one rebels against the other. Such adolescents are mostly those who pose as poets. They start quarrelling and criticising others. The parents should be cautious of their such wards who pose to be poets, because such poets are very sensitive and emotional.

Parents should also see that their wards do not establish friendship with much older persons because the social and emotional ways of older persons are not conducive for the developing life of adolescents and their influence proves a hurdle in their desirable and healthy development.

SUMMARY

Friendship is a must in an individual's life. An adolescent should exercise caution in the selection of friends. The parents should also help him in the selection of good friends otherwise it is possible that he may cultivate friendship with undesirable persons.

Adolescents by nature want to make friendship with those who are their equals in social and economic status and in age. The adolescent is an emotional being and he quarrels with his friends at times and entertains a feeling of jealousy.

Adolescents want to become a leader of their friend-circle, but only those who have an attractive personality, superior intelligence and courteous manners succeed in getting leadership. There are five type of leaders among adolescents : (1) Social leaders, (2) Intellectual leaders, (3) Leaders in extracurricular activities, (4) Games and sports leaders, and (5) All-rounders.

The leadership of adolescent is comparatively more stable than that of children because it is based on certain qualities.

Attractive physical appearance, superior intelligence, high social status, good academic career, seniority in age and impressive personality are necessary for leadership. There are many causes for the failure of friendship and important among them are physical deformity, poor social and economic position, selfishness, jealousy, geographical distance, quarrelsome nature, dullness, too much humility, too much intellectual superiority and bossism.

The reasons for success are charming physical appearance, good social and economic position, interest and sympathy with others, experience, good host, intelligence, self-control, selflessness and a sense of responsibility and ability to reach a decision early.

The parents' duty is to guide the adolescent through their own exemplary behaviour towards their friends and warn them against entering into friendship with undesirable persons.

Exercises

1. Discuss the nature of friendship during adolescence.
2. Discuss the nature of leadership traits that attract adolescents for becoming followers.
3. What are the traits for leadership during adolescence?
4. What are the causes of success and failure of friendship during adolescence?
5. Discuss the parents' duties and responsibilities in relation to friendship of their adolescent boys and girls.

Notes

1. Spaulding C.B. 'Types of Junior-College Leaders', *Social and Res.* 18, 164–168, 1933.
2. Pigors, P. 'Types of Followers', *J. Soc. Psychol.* 5. 378–383, 1934.

9

Social Behaviours during Adolescence

A human being by nature likes company and that is why he is called a social being. During infancy he does not wish to be separated from his mother, during childhood he weeps when others show indifference towards him and feels happy in company with others. It is his desire to enjoy the company of others because he feels himself to be a member of the society although he does not actually understand its meaning. This desire is not limited to children only but is present among adolescents and adults too. Social boycott is the worst kind of punishment, and therefore, everyone desires to command respect in his society. This helps an individual's social development and this process of development continues throughout the whole life. Now we shall examine the behaviour of adolescents during this process.

Desire to Participate in Social Activities

The social behaviour of the child goes on getting complicated with his development. Though no notice is taken of his social behaviour during early years, yet the parents become cautious about his social behaviour when he attains the age of ten or twelve years. When the child enters adolescence the parents become extra cautious, because during adolescence the individual moves rapidly towards maturity and every one watches his actions keenly. The adolescent undergoes revolutionary changes with the result that his responsibilities increase immensely. People now expect proper social behaviour from him and he also becomes conscious of this expectation. He desires to get respect in society and, therefore, now he participates in social works more actively.

Violent Emotional Tension

An adolescent's emotional tension increases due to his increased responsibilities as compared to those during childhood. If he fails to discharge his responsibilities successfully the tension becomes more intense. Because he is in the process of learning things, shortcomings and failures are but natural. However, the mind of adolescent is always full of apprehensions because he does not know where he may commit some mistake. Like boys, the girls' minds are also full of apprehensions because they, too, are in the same developing process, although their problems are different to those of the boys. The social behaviour expected of girls is different from those expected of boys, because they have to face different responsibilities in life. At some places boys face more difficulties and at some places the girls. Therefore, the emotional tension of girls differ from that of the boys. Emotional tension intensifies with increase in the area of social behaviour. Adolescent's feelings towards his companions, teachers and near and dear ones become deeper. A child when snubbed by some one who is dear to him feels hurt and he wants to extend his affection towards that individual who loves him. The child as compared to the adolescent soon adjusts himself with the new situation. An adolescent frequently quarrels because he comes in contact with various persons in discharge of his social responsibilities. Moreover, he is also not in a position to fully discharge his responsibilities. It is, therefore, that he takes more time to adjust himself as compared to a child. This naturally means that emotional tension of an adolescent is more intense and lasts longer.

Correction during Childhood Necessary for Proper Social Behaviours

For expecting desirable social behaviour from an adolescent it is necessary to guide him from childhood because the roots of social behaviour are found during childhood. If the social behaviour during childhood is not satisfactory, the behaviour during adolescence will generally be far from satisfactory and it will be difficult to correct him at this stage. It is not necessary that with physical development an adolescent also becomes socially mature. Therefore, the social behaviour should be watched from childhood and corrected whenever necessary. Those parents who enjoy or take pleasure in unsocial behaviour of their sons and daughters during their childhood face difficulties in correcting the same when they reach adolescence. Everything has to pass through the development process and nothing grows all of a sudden. So behaviour of adolescent takes root during childhood and care should be taken at the very stage to put it on the right track. A child who does not learn proper social behaviour grows selfish during adolescence. He may dislike others' company and develop inferiority complex. He will indulge in day-dreams and will be unaware of the realities of life. Here, therefore, lies the importance of teaching correct social behaviour during childhood.

Helping the Adolescent to Adopt Better Manner

Correcting the social behaviour during childhood does not mean that the adolescent's problems of social behaviour are solved. It is simply a helping process. The adolescent faces new problems of social behaviour and it is difficult to get an indication of them during childhood. It is possible that the problem that does not worry an individual during childhood may cause great headache during adolescence. He may be a successful leader of his group during childhood, but he may not be so during adolescence. He, therefore, needs new directions. The adolescent should be as far as possible saved from bitter social experiences and should be helped in avoiding ugly and humiliating social experiences. If it is not done, he will suffer from inferiority complex and will lack courage in facing difficult situations. Care should be taken to save the adolescent from undesirable tendencies.

Social Influence during Adolescence

Every one has an impact of social influence, but the impact is more in the case of adolescents. Social consciousness is not much during childhood and the individual is not much capable of understanding happenings around himself. But this is not so with an adolescent who understands the environment more now. He, therefore, is more influenced by his environment. The social influence is more abiding on the adolescent, because he is now more keen to learn various things for solving his difficulties and it is difficult to obliterate the effect of what he learns in his keenness. There are other impacts also besides learning something. Impact of inferiority complex is one such thing. If an adolescent is rebuked from time to time or if his ability is questioned frequently he develops a sense of inferiority complex. This should be avoided, because it is very difficult to make him acquire self-confidence when once he loses it.

Widening Friend-Circle

The adolescent comes in contact with numerous persons. Thus his circle of friends widens. During childhood an individual's activities are mostly confined to the house or neighbourhood, but an adolescent's activities take place in comparatively much wider area. He also wants to come in contact with a large number of people. He is also keen to know what others think about him. This desires prompts him to come in contact with others. How much influence he will exercise ever a person or a group depends upon the depth of his relationship with the parties concerned. During childhood an individual's intimate relationship is confined to the members of the family or playmates. The number of bosom friends is less. During adolescence the number of intimate friends increase.

Giving Importance to Social Views

The adolescent attaches great importance to reactions of the society and is very careful about his own and to others behaviour. He is always eager to learn the behaviour which is appreciated. He, therefore, tries to copy respectable and well recognised personalities. With a view to getting appreciation from others, he learns the traditional behaviour of others. Evidently, he now attaches great importance to the reactions of society. He honours the decisions of society because he is not very sure about the correctness of his own decisions. However, this state of affairs is not permanent. Gradually he learns proper social behaviour and develops his own personality. He, therefore, starts asserting his personality. If, however, his assertion fails he becomes timid.

Expectations from the Society in General

With growth in social consciousness, the adolescent tries to mould his character and behaviour according to accepted social traditions and values. He tries to find out what exactly the society expects from him. This is natural because even a child of eight or ten years realises some social responsibilities and tries to become obedient, honest and cooperative. He realises that his capabilities are limited so he should not indulge into tall talks before others. The adolescent being comparatively more mature knows these things better than a child.

He accordingly tries to prove himself and in so doing he wants to serve those near to him in the society. When he does not get appreciation from the society for his efforts, he gets hurt and he stops serving the society.

Tendency of Self-Display

Gradually the adolescent gets some measure of self-confidence and desires to be respected. He now thinks that he can stand on his own legs and, therefore, in order to impress this fact on others he tries to attract their attention. This tendency generally appears during middle adolescence and occasionally taken an ugly shape. He wants to express this feeling anywhere, and everywhere without caring for any manner. He displays this tendency in many ways like putting on brightly coloured garments, laughing loudly, speaking with a false air of authority on a subject on which his knowledge is shallow, strange pronunciation of words, giving assertive opinion on disputed issues, walking in a peculiar manner, using bombastic words, criticising others, giving lessons to others, boasting about any of his successes etc. Gradually, it dawns on him that others do not like this sort of behaviour on his part and then he tries to mend himself. In this effort he comes to know as to what is acceptable to the society and what is detested by it.

Quarrels during Adolescence

Quarrelling with others is a part of human being's nature. Children, adolescents, adults and nations quarrel amongst themselves. This is present in an individual since childhood. Children quarrel for petty things like toys, dresses, edibles etc. The reasons behind adolescents' quarrel is mostly social. If an adolescent wants to dominate others quarrel takes place. Ill treatment also ends in quarrel. Jealousy or anger are also causes of quarrels. If a boy is ill treated in the home while the other is treated in a better manner, the ill treated boy will burst into anger and jealousy and will start quarrelling. He not only quarrels with those of his age group but also quarrels with his father, mother, brothers and others. The boys are more quarrelsome during childhood, but during adolescence it is the girls who quarrel more. It is also observed that adolescents would like to settle their dispute among themselves, but girls will invite the third party to mediate. The ways of quarrel among adolescents are many for instances abusing, chiding, hot discussions and condemning before others. Unlike children, the quarrels of adolescents last longer and they do not easily forgive and forget. Despite great efforts for compromise, the anger is not easily subdued and it lingers on for long.

Protesting against Elders' Control

The authority and control of elders is resented equally by children and adolescents. The difference is only in the degree. The resentment of adolescent is stronger. They even go to the length of breaking the relationship and run away from the home. The parents rebuke their wards for certain bad habits like disobedience, late returning to home, eating spiced stale food in the market or going to cinemas in company with undesirable elements. The parents do not want to relax their control over their wards in order to save them from these evils, but the adolescent does not like parents' interference in his affairs. He threatens to leave the house when his demands are not met. The girls, of course, resort to weeping, disobedience and calling names. Adolescents resent any kind of punishments. Some flatter the parents and many hide the real facts to win them over. If they succeed in their designs they boast of befooling their parents. Sometimes they become so impertinent as to openly tell their parents that they better understand their affairs and they (parents) need not poke their nose in their affairs. The girls in India do not protest much against parent's control because in our country girls do not enjoy much freedom. However, in European and American countries where girls enjoy equal freedom their protest is strong and they display temperament like that of boys.

Considering themselves Great or Small on the Basis of Caste, Colour and Appearance

A child even during his childhood has a feeling of superiority against some and also feeling of inferiority against some others. This is due to the position and influence of the family. This feeling takes stronger roots during adolescence. The cause of entertaining such a feeling may be due to caste, colour, physical appearance or the position in the society. The adolescent who are fair complexioned and are good looking consider themselves superior to those who are not so endowed. This feeling is stronger in girls. They in their heart silently compare their beauty with that of other girls and if they find themselves inferior to others they develop inferiority complex. This feeling gets so deep-rooted that even after their marriage they are not able to overcome it. There are many mothers, too, who compare their daughter's beauty and qualities with other girls in an unpsychological manner. This adversely affects the girls. The impact of caste, colour and beauty is also visible in boys too, and accordingly they consider themselves superior or inferior. This feeling gets working since early childhood. The boys who consider themselves superior behave redely with others. The blame for this undesirable behaviour lies more on the family environment than on the boys themselves. They are taught to behave in that fashion. Among the adolescents besides the family influence, the boys themselves wilfully exhibit contempt for others whom they consider inferior. They even show contempt towards their younger brothers and sisters or companions who are ugly or considered inferior in some other respect. This is an undesirable trait and adversely affects an adolescent's personality and character.

Categories of Adolescent's Acquaintances

An adolescent's behaviour changes. He appears to be somewhat unsocial, because his interest in his childhood playmates declines. He prefers to remain aloof and also does not want to mix up with other grown up individuals. This mental state is a temporary phase because with further physical development he again starts taking interest in social activities. Now he starts searching friends according to his liking. In other words, he wants to make his own new society. During adolescence the parents are more worried about their children for saving them from bad company and keep them on the right track. The adolescent is, therefore, often rebuked and snubbed. The parents superficially appear to be less affectionate. In these circumstances, the adolescent wants to carve out such a society where he can get affectionate behaviour and respect from others. We have already mentioned earlier that friendship of adolescent is more stable than the friendship of children. Adolescents come in contact with various persons, but are never in haste to make friends. The depth of friendship of an adolescent may be divided into the following five categories :

(i) To know a person by name but not getting and opportunity to meet him.
(ii) Formal introduction with a person once or twice.
(iii) Meeting a person often, but not having particular affection for him.
(iv) Although friendship has been established, but has not been taken into confidence.
(v) Very intimate friendship in which confidence may be reposed in him or her and he or she can open his or her mind without any fear of betrayal.

Behaviour with Intimate Friends

The number of friends vary with each adolescent. Some may have only one intimate friend, while the other may have more than one. Besides, it is also possible that the number of friends increase or decline according to sentiments, feelings and development. An adolescent may also possess different intimate friends for different environments and situations. His intimate friend in his locality may be some one and in the class another person. Intimate friendship continues for a long period. It is also seen that friends of childhood continue to be life long friends. Quarrels or differences of opinion also occur among intimate friends, but soon after they talk frankly and remove misunderstanding.

Friends also change according to needs and development. Friendship during early adolescence may differ from the friendship of middle adolescence or that of middle adolescence from that during late adolescence. In such a situation, the individual tries to establish friendship with others and if he fails in this venture he indulges in day-dreams and becomes sentimental. The intimate friendship of girls is stronger than that of boys. The girl's friends open up their hearts before each other and do not hide their secrets. This is generally not the case with boys who hide their secrets often from their intimate friends.

CLUB LIFE DURING ADOLESCENCE

Both during childhood and adolescence the boys and girls form a group or a club of five or six. The clubs of adolescents are on more permanent footing because their interests do not change so frequently as those of children. During childhood when an aim of the club is achieved the club is dissolved and new clubs with new members for a new purpose may be formed. During the adolescence, clubs are formed with more solid purposes and adolescents are more faithful to the moral purposes and policies. The purpose of clubs during adolescence is mostly social while during childhood the purpose is purely personal, because children like to play games involving courage. In these daring acts of games they often incur the displeasure of neighbours. The adolescents, on the other hand, keep regard of neighbours' convenience and do not try to annoy them. They act with greater understanding. The main purpose of adolescents' clubs may be conversation and games.

Games during Adolescence

Holliganism is not a part of the games of adolescents. Their main games are cricket, football, hockey, volleyball, badminton, gulli-danda, basketball, carom, chess etc. An adolescent enjoys the company of friends more than the game itself. In games he is happy because he is away from the control of elders. We have already discussed other forms of adolescents' games in an earlier chapter.

Adolescents' Conversations in Club

The conversations or discussions in an adolescents' club cover a wide range of subjects. They are mostly unplanned and may embrace subjects of social, national or international importance. They may say whatever comes on their tongue. They may also criticise each other without any bad motives behind and, therefore, no body is hurt by such a criticism. Some adolescents who are more influential try to dominate the conversation and if in so doing he wants to impress others, then the other boys turn a deaf ear towards his utterances. They also do not give him opportunity to speak much. However, this much credit may be allowed to adolescents that despite criticism of each other no one feels ill and everyone tries to extent affectionate behaviour towards the other. The question of some one being considered high or low does not arise in a club.

Usefulness of a Club for Adolescents

An adolescent stands to benefit in many ways from club-participation. He gets experience of varied subjects and come in contact with many persons. He also comes to know his real worth. He also derives satisfaction by participating in a club. If he happens to be feeling irritated due to parents' or guardian's behaviour the club provides him solace. Besides he generally enjoys healthy entertainment at a club. Entertainment is very necessary for mental health. A child derives pleasure even in home playing with his toys or with parents, but the adolescent needs something else. In a club the adolescent learns finer points of social behaviour. It is there that he realises what kind of behaviour should be extended to different individuals. This immensely helps him in adjusting in the environment. He also learns the quality of tolerance and its worth in real life. The club life also enable him to assess the worth of an individual's character and nature which is very necessary for a successful life. Similarly, through club life he learns the worth of mutual help, sacrifice and co-operation.

Harmful Effects

Clubs are not always beneficial to adolescents. They have a darker side as well. An adolescent may develop such a great passion for club that he may become indifferent towards other responsibilities. There are many adolescents who neglect studies and house-work and devote more time to club programmes. A member of the club may also develop a sense of superiority and contempt for non-members. Those individuals who are not popular in club are laughed at by the popular members of the club. This develops a feeling of inferiority complex.

Effect of Clubs on Adolescents

Club life greatly influences an adolescent's character, because this is a phase of life when others behaviour and views very easily influence the adolescent. He learns the style of hair-dressing, conversation, putting on certain type of dresses during adolescence. Besides, his moral, social and religious views are also formed in this phase of life. Thus we see that clubs may exercise great influence over adolescents.

Clubs More Common in Boys

Clubs are more common in boys as compared to girls. The reason is that in current social environment boys are more free as compared to girls. The girls cannot afford so much time for club because of social traditions and restrictions. Moreover, they have special responsibilities of sharing the household work with their mothers. Consequently their field of social activities is very limited.

SOME PROBLEMS RELATING TO SOCIAL LIFE OF ADOLESCENTS

Impatient Behaviour

An adolescent shows impatience in his behaviour. His power of copying others in strong like children. So he tries to emulate the behaviour of elders. But he is so impatient that he sometimes crosses the limit. He jumps in a work for immediate satisfaction. He is at this stage unmindful of consequences.

Desire to Reform the Society

The adolescent tries to bring reform in society according to his own thinking. He feels gloomy about the prevailing evil practices in the society. Sometimes he gets fully prepared to remove them. This is really a healthy sign because it prompts him to go ahead to achieve higher ideals.

Adverse Effects of Elders' Policy of Double Standards

It has already been mentioned in an earlier chapter that adolescents want to take part in various games and social activities in accordance with the various developmental stages they happen to pass through. For this purpose they want full freedom. They also try to find opportunity for this purpose. And when they do not get this opportunity, they get highly dissatisfied and also occasionally violate social traditions. Elders preach them lessons of honesty and devotion to duty, but when they find them using double standards they get irritated. This double standard gives birth to inner conflicts in them. The policy of parents to make them follow what they preach but not to practise themselves accordingly creates resentment in adolescents. Whenever the adolescent retorts that he is simply following the elders, the elders sarcastically remark "Imitate us only when you become like us. Why do you not look to our good qualities and why do you try to imitate our weaknesses only". This snubbing adversely affects the adolescents. Parents and teachers must not lose sight of the fact that an adolescent's social adjustment is deeply related to his adjustment in home and schools and as such if he is unable to successfully adjust himself in the home and school he will then not be able to adjust himself in the society. It is commonly observed that an adolescent who has successfully adjusted himself in the home and the school also adjusts himself in the society and he is able to exercise self-control in his social behaviour.

Providing Opportunities for the Development of Social Qualities

It is necessary to give opportunities to the adolescent for sharing some social responsibilities. He himself desires to participate in social activities and, therefore, it will be only proper to provide him occasions to fulfil his desire. This will automatically solve some of his problems. Efforts should be made to set up such centres where adolescents may gather and take part in agreed programmes. Such adolescents centres will help the development of his constructive approach to different subjects and they will also learn the worth of collective work. Such centres may be opened in schools, temples, houses, church or other places near these religious centres. The aims of these centres may be as follows :

(1) Organising healthy entertainment to pass leisure.
(2) Development of leadership for some specific purpose.
(3) To get opportunity to develop contacts with other members of the society.

In these centres adolescents of the same age group may be combined to develop various qualities but the job of developing and acquiring qualities should not be left alone to adolescents. The parents should themselves take interest and inspire them to develop moral and social values. The parents should allow their wards to hold meetings at the home occasionally to which he may be allowed to invite his friends. Such occasions also give an opportunity to parents and guardians to know the aptitudes and tendencies of their adolescents.

SUMMARY

The human being is a social animal and possesses a born desire to participate in social activities. He desires company and feels gloomy aloof. As he grows, his social behaviour becomes complex. He tries to command respect in the society. During adolescence the pace of development is rapid and the desire to participate in social activities is very strong. At this age the adolescent has an intense emotional tension and he takes comparatively longer time than children or adult in overcoming it. It is the duty of parents to properly teach social behaviour to children. This early training proves very helpful during adolescence. An adolescent should not be treated like a child, some consideration should be shown to his views. He faces new problems. So a new approach is needed bearing in mind that society has a great influence over the adolescent.

The adolescents want to increase their friend circle and are careful about the views of the society. They also feel that society expects some duties from them and they try to mould themselves accordingly. However, the tendency of self-display is strong at this stage and sometimes it takes an ugly turn. During adolescence the boys and girls develop a tendency of rebelling against elders' control and they also resort to quarrelling not only amongst themselves, but with their parents and teachers too. The adolescent's mind is also full of complexes about beauty, skin complexion and caste and they consider themselves superior or inferior accordingly.

Club play a vital role in an adolescent's life and help in the development of many virtues. In the club they discuss subjects of social, national and international importance. Club life has also its darker side. It often makes the adolescents indifferent towards other responsibilities.

There are also some problems in the social life of adolescents and important among them are : (1) rashness of behaviour and unmindfulness of consequences, (2) desire to reform the society, and (3) double standard of elders.

It is the duty of parents to give adolescents ample opportunity of correcting and learning social behaviour. They should themselves take interest and guide them in a psychological manner.

Exercises

1. Discuss the nature of social behaviour during adolescence.
2. Describe the nature of friendship during adolescence.
3. Discuss the nature of club life during adolescence.
4. Describe the nature of problems relating to social life during adolescence.

10

Feelings about Sex Matters during Adolescence

Sex Feelings Develop since Childhood

Sex feelings take their roots in some form or the other since very early stage of life. The development of sex feelings give birth to many problems and it is difficult to solve all of them during childhood. Sex feelings like knowing things related to sex, love, masturbation or hunger for sexual intercourse start even when an individual is a child of eight or ten years of age or even much earlier and if these problems are tackled in a psychological manner it proves of immense help to the child when he becomes an adolescent and faces sex problems. But in India it is generally observed that parents pay very little attention to children's sex feelings. This leads the adolescent to go to undesirable companions for satisfying or getting information about his sex problems. This adversely affects the development of his personality. He develops the complex of fear, gloominess and shyness. A sex complex develops in him which is difficult to remove. Such an individual's behaviour has an imprint of sex complex. Happiness becomes a dream for him.

'Self' Attains a New Standard

The sex problems of an adolescent are highly complicated and difficult because genital organs reach the maximum development during this stage. The problems and requirements of an adolescent differ with those of children as far as sex matters are concerned. In an adolescent revolutionary psychological changes occur with the full development of his or her genital organs. He gets sentimental and is overpowered by shyness not daring to come face to face with others. The boys and girls form opinions about themselves. Thus they attain a new standard of 'self'.

Desire to Win Others' Appreciation

The attraction of boys and girls towards each other now takes a different shape from the one that existed earlier during childhood. During childhood a spirit of competition dominates them and they want to achieve victory over each other but during adolescence this feeling undergoes a change. Now they want to win appreciation and approval of the opposite sex.

Lack of Proper Guidance Harmful in Sex-Matters

It is a general feeling of parents in our country that boys and girls acquire sex knowledge automatically and they need no guidance. This is a wrong view and if proper guidance is not given to boys and girls in this matter they stand to suffer and face innumerable difficulties in future life. The attraction of boys and girls towards each other does not start all of a sudden. It is a gradual process and takes time. If boys and girls are not taught social behaviour towards each other they then have to face a lot of difficulties and despite full development men and women lack frankness in their behaviour towards each other and also do not feel encouraged in doing a work with a collective or team spirit. It is also generally observed that men and women feel shy in expressing their views frankly before each other. Sometimes speaking of a sentence or two becomes a difficult task. The main reason behind this hesitation is lack of proper education during adolescence. Boys and girls in such circumstances resort to other sources to give vent to their feelings and achieve satisfaction. They may, in this pursuit for satisfaction develop the habit of day-dreams or reading of romantic novels. This results into a lop-sided development of an individual's personality and creation of difficulties in future life.

Boys and Girls to get Opportunity of Mixing Together in a Healthy Environment

Co-education, according to many psychologists, is a correct step to remove the above feeling of frustration among boys and girls, although it is difficult to say how far this programme may succeed in India under the present social conditions. According, to this programme boys and girls of equal age and social status should be given opportunity of mixing with each other in healthy and open environment. This will help in removing wrong ideas and feelings entertained by boys and girls towards each other and they may acquire some such experience which may be necessary for happy future life.

Sympathetic Attitude of Parents and Teachers Necessary

It is the responsibility of teachers, and parents to make arrangements to impart that knowledge and information which the adolescent needs for satisfying curiosities and feelings related to sex matters. The parents must take interest in knowing the mental condition of their boys and girls and adopt a sympathetic and helpful attitude in solving their problems. The adolescents should get a feeling of confidence that they are free to consult any one about their sex problem as and when necessity arises. This will give immense satisfaction to them and at the same time will help the parents to adopt helpful attitude towards adolescents' problems. Some parents feel shy in explaining sex matters to their adolescents. They appear so morally weak on this point that it seems that they themselves suffer from some sort of sex complex. In order to give the country healthy and morally strong generation the parents of the present-day should throw away the veil of shyness and extend reasonable help to adolescents.

Unsympathetic Attitude creates Feeling of Shyness

Sympathetic attitude in this matter is of vital importance because it gives adolescents satisfaction and satisfies his curiosities and helps in the correct development of his personality. Unsympathetic attitude is a curse on the adolescents, because it gives birth to feeling of shyness, hesitation and immorality which in course of time gets deep rooted. It then requires the help of competent psychologist in helping the adolescent to get rid of these evils.

What Excites Sex Feelings

There are certain factors which generate sex feeling in an adolescent. Physical development alone is not sufficient to excite sex feelings. These excitements are as follows :

(1) Romantic and sex dominating music.

(2) Naked body of male or female.
(3) Obscene literature.
(4) Pictures of naked women and men.
(5) One's own body.
(6) Dance.
(7) Sexual Conversation.
(8) Excitement created by riding an animal.
(9) Cinema.
(10) Obscene picture or pornography.
(11) Mental prostitution.
(12) Seeing animals in compromising pose or their road-side sexual acts.

Sex Problems of Unmarried Adolescents

Urban adolescents who are not married face many problems related to sex during unmarried life. Although the development of matters related to sex start from childhood, yet the problems are different at the various stages of development. The most difficult sex problem is faced by urban unmarried adolescents who though become sexually mature, yet are socially immature because they have not yet completed education in order to become an earning and independent members of the society. In such a situation he is not in a position to get married and satisfy his sexual curiosities and urges. The case of a rural adolescents in India is somewhat different, because their parents get them married when they attain the age of 17 or 18 years. Rural adolescents, therefore, do not face such difficult problems. But those in the urban areas who have to depend on service for their livelihood have to face certain problems. The urban adolescents do not try to get married before they are in a position to carry out the financial responsibility of a married life. They in this aspect resemble with adolescents of some advanced foreign countries like U.S.A. and Europe. This gives rise to many pre-marital sex problems and their difficulties also increase many times because of sex excitement in the social environment surrounding them. Films, novels, magazines, prostitutes and society girls and literature relating to birth control constitute such sex excitements. An unmarried adolescent is likely to face problems concerning: (i) masturbation and mental prostitution, (ii) homo-sexuality, the adolescent in this state of mind has little interest in the opposite sex, (iii) love with opposite sex and problems related to it, and fear of social criticism, (iv) unable to satisfy sexual desires in the natural way, may lead the adolescent in search of different kinds of luxuries.

Some Other Difficulties

Because of shyness during adolescence boys and girls face some other kind of problems besides those mentioned above. Physical deformity of some kind is a serious problem for those adolescents who have made various attempts in hiding them. There are many physical deformities including small pox marks, defective eyes, deformities of legs or hands, too much dark complexion or too lean or too fat. Some have six fingers. Any of these deformities create a sense of inferiority complex. The girls are particularly worried about deformities because of unhappy marriage prospects. People also pass uncharitable remarks. The parents, too, get much frustrated while looking for a bridegroom. This frustration also develops a sense of inferiority complex in the parents and it is difficult for them to overcome it.

Love Problems and Ideals Develop since Childhood

In the early years the child is absorbed in himself and does not feel the need of any companion. This is the view of Hurlock[1]. Only after attaining the age of six or seven years the boys and girls desire to play in the company of each other. After this age boys and girls like to play in the company of those belonging to their sex. A spirit of competition appears in the boys and girls at the age of ten or twelve years and they try to belittle each other. Again after the age of thirteen or fourteen years the boys and girls are attracted towards each other. Thus we find an order in the attraction of boys and girls. According to Butterfield[2] boys and girls are attracted towards each other unconsciously since childhood. During adolescent the desire of boys and girls coming in contact with each other gets strong and also becomes apparent. Both sexes create an ideal of love. This ideal starts taking shape since early childhood. It is, of course, possible that the boys and girls are not aware of its existence. True love at first sight will not have been a psychological truth if there did not exist this pre-determined ideal before the adolescent according to Butterfield.

Lack of Mutual Interest among Boys and Girls during Early Adolescence

During early adolescence sometimes there is a lack of mutual attraction and they are indifferent towards each other. They also try to show contempt towards each other. The boys consider girls as foolish, weaklings and inferior. Similarly girls consider boys as loafers, discourteous, cruel and uncivilised. This feeling occasionally gets so strong that girls consider each member of the opposite sex in the same terms. They even do not spare their fathers and shower these objectives on them in jokes. Similarly boys go to the extent of calling their mothers as foolish, weak and inferior in human qualities. This brings before the parents a strange situation relating to discourteous behaviour of adolescents. Such boys and girls whose relations with the members of the family during childhood had been affectionate never create such problems. Fortunately the feeling of contempt which overpowers the individuals during early adolescence disappears after a year or so because within this period the genital organs develop rapidly and change comes in the outlook of adolescents. In the Indian social set-up the male enjoys more freedom and therefore this development is comparatively easier and smooth among boys, but the girls attitude takes a longer time to change. This might be due to their different role and responsibilities during the future life.

Reasons for Lack of Interest in Boys and Girls

The differentiation stressed in the role and responsibilities adversely affects the girls and the reasons for mutual lack of interest are mostly social. In India every now and then girls are told not to do this or that or not to behave in this or that manner because that kind of behaviour is the special prerogatives of boys. For instance, in schools and colleges some special subjects like domestic science or music are recommended to girls, while agriculture or mathematics are recommended to boys. This kind of differentiation creates a feeling of inferiority complex in girls and superiority complex in boys. Moreover, whatever is indirectly told about sex problems by the parents is such as to generate a feeling of inferiority complex in girls. The girls start thinking that they occupy an inferior place in the family and the society. Problems and difficulties relating to menstruation and childbearing also leave a bad effect with the result that they (girls) consider themselves second rate and unfortunate in the society. The girls envy the lot of boys and their indifference becomes all the more stronger. However, a psychological approach on the part of parents on these matters may make all the difference and the girls may get mentally prepared cheerfully to shoulder their future responsibilities. Cinemas, novels etc., depicting male characters favourably also create a sense of indifference towards the opposite sex in girls. Better behaviour towards male members in the family or society is another factor. Father's cruelty towards children is yet another reason. Such things may sometimes create permanent contempt towards menfolk in girls.

Impact of Disinterestedness on Behaviour

The above disinterestedness has serious repercussions on the behaviour of boys and girls. Their behaviour towards each other becomes rude. They are unhelpful to each other. They will not join a function where the members of other sex are also expected to be present. They also leave no effort unspared in belittling each other.

Two Pictures of Love during Middle Adolescence

The adolescent in the middle stage has two pictures of love. An individual's genital organs get fully developed by middle adolescence. His physical appearance also looks better. His mental condition also improves and instead of indulging in day-dreams he prefers remaining on solid ground. During this period he develops two types of love. According to the first, he loves a member of the same sex; and according to the other, he develops love for a member of the opposite sex.

Pure Love with the Same Sex

An individual wants some kind of outlet for his feelings and when he develops indifference for a member of the opposite sex the need for such an outlet becomes more acute. He then tries to love an individual belonging to his own sex. This love is extended to an individual who may be senior in age and superior in qualities. The adolescent is attracted towards this individual on finding himself lacking in these qualities. This gives him immense satisfaction. An adolescent boy admires other successful boys. These successful boys may be his classmates or schoolmates. They may also admire or make a film hero or national leader an object of love. By doing so they feel that they are developing masculine qualities. This is also inspiring for the boys and this behaviour is quite natural for adolescents. This kind of behaviour also helps in the development of mental, moral and idealistic values. But if this kind of love persists even after adolescence, it indicates that the adolescent is mentally immature and lacks self-confidence. An adolescent enjoys this love and tries to follow his ideal. He feels very happy in his company and expresses his appreciation through letters and poems.

Love with High Regard and Hero-Worship of Individual Belonging to the Opposite Sex

The indifference towards members of the opposite sex gradually disappears when genital organs of adolescents attain maturity. The boys and girls now show interest in each other and try to know each other's secrets. They are attracted towards each other but there is a veil of social obstacles and shyness between them which prevent the fulfilment of their desires. They, therefore, indulge in mental prostitution and their imagination of sexual things run riot. They also develop respectful love for elderly people of the opposite sex. This senior individual belongs to his environment and could be a teacher, friend, neighbour, social leader, an actor or an actress. They become the adolescents object of love. Indian youths these days are so much enamoured of actors and actresses that they feel flattered in offering their love to them. These boys and girls try to emulate them in all walks of life and waste their time and energy.

Hero-Worship — Future Emotional Experience

Such hero-worship in many cases is for individuals who are not personally known to boys and girls. The hero himself does not know that he is being worshipped by some one. But of course, there are many such individuals who encourage younger people to flatter them. They derive pleasure from such a flattery by others. Hero-worship is rather a distant affair and society does not appreciate it. Hero-worshippers are mostly condemned and are considered object of contempt. However, the hero of the youth exercises a lot of emotional influence and young boys and girls do not tolerate those who criticise them on this score. He also feels deeply injured when there are indications that their hero has no affection for him. He becomes restless and is unable to concentrate on work. Sometimes, the emotional impact is so devastating that he contemplates of committing suicide.

Desire to Meet the Opposite Sex during Middle Adolescence

Although the Indian society unlike the Western one does not permit freedom to adolescents to mix freely with members of the opposite sex, yet there is a strong natural desire among adolescents during middle adolescence to come in intimate contact with members of the opposite sex. This desire of intimate contact is born a bit earlier in girls because they mature a bit earlier than boys do. In boys this desire appears at the age of 17 or 18 years. Social restrictions make it difficult for the adolescent to express this feeling but writings and behaviours do indicate the presence of this feeling in adolescents. Following the girls going to schools and colleges and thus wasting a lot of physical and mental energy is an example of this kind of behaviour although they face numerous difficulties in such pursuits. These difficulties may be the following :

(i) Social fear. The adolescent wants to do this secretly and avoids being seen by others for fear of social condemnation and contempt;
(ii) Fear of being made fun of by the friends; and
(iii) Fear of punishment and snubbing by teachers, parents or relations of the opposite sex.

Pitiable Condition of Educated Indian Adolescent

The adolescent passes through a difficult and pitiable stage in life during this period. He is so much engrossed in this pursuit that it affects his studies. He is unable to concentrate on his studies and is always mentally engaged in finding ways to fulfil his desire. This type of behaviour of his is condemned in the present day Indian society, and it cannot be said what will be the attitude of the society in future. However, this much may be said that the present attitude of the society towards this problem is not in the interest of the future life of the adolescent. Marriages arranged between unknown boys and girls have produced bad results. The condition of educated adolescent is all the more pitiable because the society does not allow them to develop intimate contacts with opposite sex. Parents arrange marriages according to their personal views and interests. All this results into unhappy married life. However, this much may be said that the unhappiness of married life is not entirely caused by the fact that two unknown human beings were married. If this had been the sole reason for unhappy married life in India, then no unhappy married life would have been present in western countries and so much emphasis on divorce would not have been laid there. However, some pre-introduction is essential before youths are married and this could certainly contribute towards happier married life.

SUMMARY

Feelings about Sex Matters during Adolescence

Feelings about sex matters take their root in some form or the other during childhood and they go on developing gradually. A psychological approach is needed on the part of parents, otherwise complexes develop. During adolescence when genital organs develop the adolescent undergoes a psychological change and if at this stage he is not properly and sympathetically guided many problems may arise in his future life.

During adolescence the boys and girls become shy and this shyness may be overcome if they are provided with a healthy environment. Physical development no doubt gives birth to sexual desires, but there are many other stimulants which impart keenness to sexual desires. The stimulants are, romantic music, naked body of girl or of boy, pornographic and obscene literature, own body, obscene films, pictures, dances, riding an animal or witnessing sexual acts of animals.

The unmarried youth has to face a number of problems such as masturbation, homosexuality, fear of condemnation of society and resorting to other devices in the absence of non-satisfaction of natural desire. Besides these difficulties, there are other problems which they have to face. Physical deformity of some kind is the most important among them.

The ideal of love develops in an order. At one age the child desires no company, then he desires company irrespective of sex; again he likes to play with members of his own sex. Sometimes during early adolescence the boys and girls show no interest in each other. But during middle adolescence there is a strong attraction for intimate contact with the opposite sex.

In the Indian social environment the boys and girls are not permitted to mix up freely. This gives rise to hero-worship or creates affection for a senior person of the same sex.

The condition of educated Indian adolescent is pitiable because social tradition come as a hurdle in the fulfilment of his natural desire. Marriages are arranged by parents and these mostly prove a failure.

Some pre-introduction should be permitted between boys and girls who are going to be married. This may contribute to a large extent in making married life happier.

Exercises

1. Discuss the adolescent's feelings relating to matters concerning sex.
2. What should the parents do for making the life of the adolescent more well-adjusted regarding their married life.?
3. Describe the nature of feeling of adolescent boys and girls towards each other.
4. What are the sex problems of unmarried youths in our Indian Society ?
5. Discuss the nature of love for the opposite sex during adolescence.

Notes

1. Hurlock, E.B. *Adolescent Development*, p. 401, Mc. Graw-Hill Book Company, Inc., New York, First Edition, 1949.
2. Butterfield, O.M., 'Love Problems of Adolescence' *Teach. Coll Contr., Educ.*, No. 768, 1939.

11

Some Difficulties of Newly Married Couples

FEAR OF CONDEMNATION BY SOCIETY A BIG HURDLE IN THE FULFILMENT OF NATURAL DESIRES

The structure of present day Indian society is such that newly married couples find it difficult to satisfy many of their natural and legitimate desires. Whereas in the Western society courtship precedes marriage and the couples fully know each other, here in India courtship begins after the marriage. It is the natural desire of the new couple to appear beautiful before each other and impress one another with one's beauty, dress and neatness but the fear of rebuke from elders prevent them from doing so. Some elderly ladies even go to the extent of saying that they do not wish their daughter-in-laws to appear like dancing girls. The husband, too, has either to depend on parents for money or his income is not enough to lead a happy life. In such circumstances an inner conflict in the hearts of husband and wife goes on raging.

EARLY DIFFICULTIES IN ROMANTIC CONVERSATION OF ADOLESCENTS

Newly wed adolescents have a natural desire to enter into romantic conversation with each other and know as much about each other as possible. The husband in the early days of married life is too much devoted to his wife provided she is not ugly or bad natured. But he does not get enough opportunity to enjoy her company. In India in rural areas the elders do not allow them to meet each other as and when they so desire. The husband gets opportunity in night only to visit his wife. He approaches her stealthily like a thief and leaves her before the dawn. The couple deeply feel such bad traditions but cannot express their resentment openly.

ADOLESCENTS HAVE NO ADEQUATE AND DESIRABLE KNOWLEDGE OF LOVE-MAKING

In the absence of necessary education of love-making the Indian couple face many embarrassments. The husband is expected to take the initiative in this respect because girls are by nature shy and, therefore, cannot take any initiative. In India generally both the boys and girls have no education in love making. Undoubtedly they want to educate themselves in this art but resources lack. Hence they seek the advice of their friends or read cheap literature on the subject. The boys and girls who get an opportunity to see romantic films do acquire some knowledge in this field but the education they receive at home in this respect is faulty and incomplete.

CRITERION OF BEAUTY

Every one has his own different criterion for judging beauty. A boy may consider a dark complexioned girl beautiful while another may despise such a girl. If the husband and wife did not happen to like each other, then their inner conflict knows no bound. A marriage is not meant for satisfying physical needs but one needs mental and spiritual peace out of marriage for real happiness. The ideal of love also differs in each adolescent and it is no wonder that an individual desires the presence of certain qualities in his would-be wife or in her would-be husband. The Indian society is such that it does not respect individual's desires on marriage matters but leaves it to chance and fate. In Western countries the condition is different and individual choose his or her life partner according to one's liking. Since this condition does not prevail in India the adolescent here face a very tough problem in this respect. The adolescents generally try to judge beauty according to the following standards :

(1) *Physical Appearance*

Some adolescent consider the facial beauty as the criterion for judging the beauty. It includes the proportionate built of nose, eyes, face, lips and complexion. Every adolescent has a different conception of beauty and his notion is formed on the basis of his thinking and experiences. It is, therefore, that some adolescents are satisfied if they get a beautiful partner with good face-cut.

(2) *Age*

Age is also a prime consideration in leading a happy married life. A boy wants his wife to be younger to him by a few years, possibly by 5 years. The girl similarly desires her husband to be a few years older. Too much difference in age does not produce true love between the husband and the wife.

(3) *Dress*

Garments and their judicious use is very important for giving an individual an attractive personality. An ugly body may appear attractive if properly attired. The manner of dressing also counts much. Fashionable dresses according to prevailing fashion increase beauty. Similarly, dressing of the hair and suitable use of arrangement are also very helpful in increasing one's beauty. Adolescents know the worth of good dress. Girls are very particular in this respect though boys appear a bit careless in matters of dress.

(4) *Intelligence and Education*

Every normal individual wants that his or her life companion should be educated and intelligent. No boy will ever like to marry an uneducated and unintelligent girl though personally he himself may not be too much educated. Of course, a less educated boy will hesitate in marrying a highly educated girl. But a less educated girl would prefer to marry a highly educated boy because she thinks that this would give her more honour and happiness. However, such couples are rarely seen enjoying a happy married life.

If a boy does not get an educated wife of his choice and if she is also not beautiful then his frustration knows no bound. He indulges in day-dreams and appears gloomy. He is so much emotionally disturbed that he may take to poetry to give vent to his sorrowful feelings. The company of such a person is mentally disturbing to others and he himself may turn into a mental patient at times.

Such adolescents lack determination of character. They always indulge into day-dreams and this makes them indolent. Unequal married life make their lives hellish. In such a situation, if a lofty ideal is not present before the adolescent and if he lacks the company of good people his downfall is a certainty. This also happens in the case of a girl. If the husband is inferior to her in beauty or quality, she does not respect him and is attracted towards other youths.

The adolescent boy also gets restless in mind in the absence of beauty and qualities in his wife. His eyes remain in search of beauty and as soon he sees a beautiful girl before him he wants to come in his intimate contact. In the real life we come across many such husbands who in order to become familiar with other women go on praising their beauty and qualities. They do not have a definite centre for satisfying their hunger for beauty. They are even attracted to all such women who are superior to their wives in some respect or the other.

Unequal married life in relation to emotions of adolescent makes him pitiable. A mental storm full of frustration and dejection rages in him. In daily life there are many occasions when his mental anguish is clearly visible. For instance, when an educated and beautiful husband having an uneducated and uncultured wife sees his companions enjoying the company of their beautiful and educated wives he gets deeply injured and feels embarrassed on such occasions. When he tries to explain some social, economic or political problems to his uneducated wife and she is unable to appreciate his efforts, he feels gloomy and disgusted. It is a great mental torture for him to put up with such a wife.

There is also a silver-lining in the dark clouds of unhappy married life. Some individuals with determination in character rise to unexpected heights when their married life is unhappy. They divert their energies to achieving lofty ideals when they do not find their conjugal life happy and they succeed because of determined and concentrated efforts. However, those with weak will power and lacking in determination instead of rising higher go steeply down the drain. But such individuals who attain unexpected heights after failing in married life are very few.

(5) *Originality*

Originality or a new type of approach also succeeds in attracting others; Adolescents try to adopt new approaches in their behaviours. They may get inspiration for the same from some novels or films. New approach in behaviour not only attracts each other but also makes a married life happy. In the absence of this originality the boys and girls feel bored of each other.

(6) *Family Environment*

If the married couple belong to equal status and come from a similar environment there is every likelihood that their married life will be happy, but if their is a big difference in status one party may consider itself superior and this may lead to lack of love between the couples. This may also create inner conflict resulting in unhappy married life. However, after adolescence when both of them understand each other a happy understanding may emerge.

(7) *Similarity in Taste*

Similarity in taste between the couple leads to happy conjugal life and dissimilarity may create obstacle in the part of true love. Every boy and girl desires that his life partner should possess similar views or be sympathetic to each other's views. In India due to lack of women's education it is difficult to get a wife educated enough according to a man's desires. Consequently, the married life is not generally happy. The couples sometimes do not express their inner desires before each other.

OBSTACLES OF THE NEWLY WEDS IN LIVING TOGETHER

The newly-wed couple want to know each other intimately and if the family conditions are not satisfactory they like to stay separately. If the boy has to go out for service or studies, the wife gets unhappy because their financial condition is not such as may enable them to live together in far away places. Even if the economic condition permits their living together, the parents and other elderly people create hurdles in their way. It is common for the mother-in-law to desire that the daughter-in-law lives with her irrespective of the feelings of the daughter-in-law. In this situation the daughter-in-law finds herself in an embarrassing position because she herself desires to live with her husband.

Desire for Self-expression

An adolescent married girl hesitates in opening her heart before her husband and needs such a companion with whom she may confide and say frankly what she thinks in her heart. In order to give expression to their inner feelings, some girls resort to diary-writing, some try to confide with another girl of her own age in the family. If they fail in these attempts they become unhappy.

JEALOUSY ALONG WITH LOVE

Generally love and jealousy go together. The depth of jealousy is in proportion to the depth of love. It is common experience that before marriage the boy loves his parents, brothers, sisters and other members of the family, but after marriage his wife becomes his centre of attraction. He may not be indifferent towards other members of his family, but by devoting major part of his time to his wife, he is left with little time to devote to others. In a sense he becomes unmindful of other members of the family. This is felt by all those who now feel neglected. They still want the same attention from him, but in not getting this they blame the new bride for her husband's neglect. Consequently, they develop a feeling of jealousy for the new bride and create difficulties in her way. They pass uncharitable remarks and inflict mental torture on her. They will neither care to look after her comforts nor will hesitate in misbehaving with her. They will also not try to understand her position and be reasonable to her. The newly married girl has to face this ugly situation with determination. If she is simple and submissive in nature she will put up with all this mental torture without much protest, but if she is also a bit strong in temperament she will protest and quarrel. This unhappy situation does not escape the notice of the young husband because the wife tells her husband about these incidents. Besides, the members of the family, too, do not take the same interest in him and become somewhat indifferent. The boy finds a difference in their behaviour. However, this situation does not last long and everyone compromises and adjusts himself with the new situation.

QUARRELS BETWEEN NEWLY-WEDS

In the above situation sometimes differences arise between the husband and the wife. The root cause of most of these disputes is that either the husband or the wife wants to reform the other. The young husband is shocked when he finds some unexpected aspect in the behaviour of his wife. He wants to reform her and often criticises her conduct. The young bride puts up with this upto some extent, but her patience has also some limit. Consequently, conflicts arise. The consequences of such conflicts are still worse because later on quarrels take place on flimsy grounds. Gradually as their understanding matures they compromise with each other and try to live peacefully.

SUMMARY

A newly married couple has to face many difficult situations in their early life and they suffer a period of mental torture. They can neither freely dress themselves nor can do many other things they want to do, because of the regard of elders who in India stick to conservatism. Lack of proper education of love-making also creates some difficulty in their way and they find it difficult to come in very close contact despite their being husband and wife.

Every individual has a different standard or conception of beauty and if the wife or the husband is not in accordance with this standard, inner conflicts arise. Some judge beauty from the built of the face-cut, some from age, some give priority to the manner of putting on dress, some give preference to education and intelligence, many like originality of approach, others may go for family traditions and there are many who want their life partner to possess similar ideas and likings.

A married couple wants to live together, but sometimes economic or service conditions or higher studies make it difficult. The newly wed girl wants to express her feelings freely and therefore wants a reliable companion of her own age. Some girls try to maintain a diary and record their feelings in it.

Love and jealousy go together. When the boy is married, he devotes more time to his wife. This makes other members of the family jealous towards the new wife. They then try to create difficulties for her. Often quarrels take place between the newly-weds, when neither of them tries to reform the other, but in course of time they adjust themselves with the new situation.

Exercises

1. What are the difficulties that newly married adolescent boys and girls face in their conservative families?
2. Suggest measures that should be adopted for making the life of the married adolescents happy.

12

Religious Doubts during Adolescence

There are many methods of study of religious doubts during adolescence. We shall discuss onwards some of the chief ones of these.

Introspective and Retrospective Report Methods

Two methods known as 'introspective' and 'retrospective' are employed in assessing the religious doubts of adolescents. People recommend some sort of objective test as a better method to know the religious doubts of adolescents but such tests also do not give a correct picture. However, there are many shortcomings in introspective and retrospective report methods. In the introspective report method it is often possible that the adolescent may not be able to express his inner feelings freely. Secondly on realising that some one else will study his answers the adolescent out of shyness may not freely write down his views.

In the retrospective report method the chances are that on achieving maturity the individual may not correctly recollect his religious ideas as they existed during adolescence. Secondly, on achieving maturity his religious views also change and he may not attach the required importance and seriousness to his views of adolescence. This error renders the retrospective report method erroneous and incomplete. Much reliance may also not be placed on the reports of parents, teachers and other elderly persons because adolescents are generally not free with them in discussing religious doubts.

Diary, Poems and Letters

Efforts are also being made to understand the religious doubts of adolescents through an analysis of their dairies, poems and letters. This method also has its shortcomings because all adolescents do not engage themselves in literary pursuits. Only a small number are interested in such activities. Therefore, this method holds good in the case of only intellectually superior adolescents. Among the above three, only diary may be considered more reliable because there is no fear in the mind of adolescent of its being read by others. The diary, therefore, faithfully records the feelings of the adolescents. But how many adolescents maintain diaries ?

Questionnaire Technique

Questionnaire technique is generally employed in the objective method. There may be more than one answer to the question and the adolescent is required to give one answer according to his thinking. A few examples of such questions are given below :-

1. Do you think that God decides things on the basis of our sins and virtues ? Yes or No
2. Is God present everywhere? Yes or No
3. An individual laboured throughout his life sincerely but he could never get two square meals. Do you think that this is an act of divine justice ? Yes or No
4. Is God willing to serve us as the mother does ? Yes or No
5. King desires flattery. Does God also desires so ? Yes or No
6. We can understand many things about God.
   (i) By studying science we may know too much _______, some ______, very little ______.
   (ii) By increasing contact with different persons we may know too much _______, some _______, very little _________.
   (iii) Through the study of philosophy we may know too much _______, some ______, very little ______.
   (iv) By praying daily we may know too much ________, some ________, very little ________.

But the difficulty in the questionnaire technique is that the questioner cannot say definitely if the adolescent has replied the questions correctly and seriously. This is also possible that the adolescent may take the questions lightly and not base his answers on personal experiences.

On the basis of this analysis we may conclude that it will not be good to depend only on one method in studying the religious doubts of adolescents. We have to use all these methods and then draw conclusions.

Religious Doubts Stronger in Adolescents

Every one needs some religious faith and he feels its necessity in one form or the other[1]. He needs religious faith to attain mental peace because during adolescence his mental condition changes rapidly and his mind remains disturbed. He considers his religious doubts of childhood incomplete. So his religious doubts get stronger and he searches for an ideal to get inspiration in order to follow the right path.

Adolescent Not Prepared to See Religious Beliefs Unrelated to Life's Problems

An adolescent wants to view religions on the basis of his experiences. He, therefore, does need so much of religious principles as he needs religious faith. He wants to realise the real element of religion and adopt it in his real life. He never cares for religious discourses. He is afraid of superstitions. His views get everyday more liberal in view of scientific development and expansion of education. An adolescent develops far more stronger reasoning power than a child and, therefore, cannot be easily persuaded like a child. He, therefore, is not ready to accept others' religious views as an authority. He does not believe in those religious principles which appear to him unrelated to the problems of real life. He is not prepared to accept and be loyal to that religion which advises him to give up worldly pleasures. But this does not mean that he becomes irreligious.

Little Interest in Religious Teachings

Adolescence is a transition period in an individual's life and all his feelings, therefore, are occasionally under the overwhelming impact of materialism sometimes says something unusual which often leave an impression that he is irreligious. But this is not true. The fact is that due to physical and mental changes his mind gets restless and he shows no interest in studying a serious subject like religion. An individual is, in fact, much interested in religious matters like God, life, death and similar other phenomena. On the surface it does appear that an adolescent ceases taking interest in religious matters, but this is not true. He can now understand more complicated religious matters and he knows it well because he thinks that by understanding religious matters his ideas will automatically become clear.

Adolescent's Beliefs based on his Early Religious Beliefs

The foundation of an adolescent's religious faith lies in his childhood's religious faith. He develops his religious thinking on the basis of his childhood's views and as such if proper guidance in this field is given to a child he will not face much difficulty during adolescence and will not need any particular reformatory step. But the parents seldom take interest in giving proper religious guidance to children. Instead, they burden them with their own religious views. Consequently, the child carries other people's burden over his shoulders and tries to lead his future life accordingly. After this development reformation in an individual's life becomes very difficult. The individual no more remains liberal in his religious views and this makes his life somewhat conservative.

Development of Emotional Instability in Adolescents

Some difference is there in the religious views of children because of their varying environments. Their conception of God differs. Their views regarding various Gods and Goddesses also differ. They also think in different terms about, prayer and worship. This realisation dawns on the individual when he becomes an adolescent. This develops some emotional instability in him and he becomes keen to know the truth.

Difference in the Religious Beliefs of Children and Adolescents

A child has no doubt in religious matters as told by others. It is only on account of curiosities that he wants to learn things about religious matters. He sees his parents and other elders worshipping God, keeping fasts and occasionally listening or participating in religious discourses. He, therefore, gets curious to know why they do so. In order to know the reason he showers a number of questions on them and very carefully listens to their replies. He never doubts them. The doubt arises only either at the end of childhood or at the beginning of adolescence. By the time the individual reaches the middle adolescence his doubts on religious matters take a firm root.

Adolescent's Efforts to find Answers to Life's Problems

The child as a matter of fact views the religion with a materialistic self-interest, whereas an adolescent's idea is to get a solution of his problem. The child wants to get something out of religion. They are taught so by the elders. He will worship only to be materially benefited.

Adolescent More Inspired from within himself

The child is motivated towards religion by copying his elders. He is not self-inspired and his worshipping is not the result of inspiration from within. However, he feels greatly flattered in worshipping the deities because in so doing he gets the appreciation of others. Contrary to this, an adolescent may take to religious worship or prayer due to an inspiration from within.

Deep Impact of Childhood Faith

Religious education is rarely imparted to children in our Indian society. Only a few families may take interest in giving religious education to their children. Consequently doubts regarding many religious matters are present. During adolescence the religious views certainly become individualistic and an individual starts analysing them with whatever intelligence he commands. However, the impact of childhood faith continues to remain during adolescence and also even later in life.

Religious Doubts during Adolescence

The real religious doubts are born during adolescence when an individual develops his reasoning power and does not accept the views of others without putting it on test on his reasoning power. The child, on the other hand, possess only a feeble reasoning power and, therefore, accepts other persons' views without analysing them. When the adolescent develops some power to analyse and understand religious matters, his interest in religion increases. This change takes place during adolescence.

Religious Doubts according to Mental Development

Psychologists differ regarding the age at which religious doubts begin. Their studies and experiments do not come to the same conclusion. Hollingworth[2] is of the opinion that when mental development of the individual reaches the age of 12 years, the religious doubt starts. At this age the individual expects reasonable answers to his questions. However, the mental age of 12 years is achieved by some children at different physical age because the pace of mental development in them is not the same.

Causes for Religious Doubts

Because of the following causes the pace of religious doubts increases during adolescence.

(1) Growth in reasoning power with the development of intelligence. Due to this development the adolescent does not accept anything like a child without arguing.
(2) A great mental change occurs when he studies various subjects in school. As a result, he deliberates over old problems with a new angle. During childhood the child without hesitation approaches his parents but during adolescence shyness does not permit him to be so frank with parents. Consequently, he is more inclined to seek the advice of teachers and friends. But they do not give him full satisfaction. He, therefore, leans towards religion to find answers for his personal problems.
(3) Development of aesthetic sense by seeing nature and artistic things also encourage leanings towards religion, because this creates a sense of respect towards God in the adolescent's mind.
(4) Social and family atmosphere may also help create religious

doubts in the adolescent. Adolescents or religious-minded families are mostly religious-minded. The students of such schools which impart religious instructions have also religious leanings.

(5) Any bitter experience in life or extreme frustration may also drive the adolescent towards religion for achieving mental peace. For instance, failure in examination or love, dangerous situation or serious illness may also generate religious feelings.

FACTORS ENCOURAGING RELIGIOUS DEVELOPMENT

Environment

Development of religious curiosity in an individual is a gradual process. It does not appear suddenly during adolescence, but it starts in some way or the other during childhood. During adolescence he only remodels his views based on the experience and knowledge gained during childhood. As the individual grows, his problems, too, multiply and he gets mentally disturbed. Consequently, in order to derive mental peace he leans towards religion. He associates his personal life more and more with religion only to attain mental peace. However, there do exist some people in whom interest for religion appears suddenly. Among these few persons, the majority belongs to adolescent girls. Gradual or sudden development of religious curiosity in an adolescent depends upon the environment. An adolescent having spent his childhood in vicious environment may develop religious curiosity all of a sudden. This may happen because of embarrassment or insult suffered due to sinful acts during childhood or it may happen for making atonements and amends for the vicious deeds. However, if the environment does not change, the adolescent may continue to remain under the impact of wrong religious beliefs acquired during childhood.

Temperament

An individual's nature also plays a vital role in the development of religious temperament. The development will be gradual and on permanent footing in the case of a peaceful and more mature individual and he may enjoy mental peace every day. But if a person is suspicious by temperament, then his emotional instability will increase with religious development because nothing will give him adequate satisfaction.

Religious Doubts Mostly arises during Adolescence

An adolescent has a better reasoning power and he accepts a thing after carefully analysing it. His reasoning power increases manifold as compared to the reasoning power he possessed during childhood when he accepted others' views without any argument. He, therefore, exercises his reasoning power to analyse what others say. If his experience is contrary to the religious beliefs, he starts entertaining doubts. It is also possible to have this kind of doubt during childhood. Intelligent children, having comparatively better developed reasoning power, may express doubts towards certain religious beliefs. But because they have little worldly experience they, therefore, do not get much disturbed. This doubt, in fact, is responsible for greater emotional instability during adolescence and the fury of this instability depends upon the background of the childhood religious life. If he had learnt religious matters with closed eyes during childhood, then it is natural to develop indifference towards them during adolescence.

Entertainment of Doubts—A Natural Process

Although entertainment of doubts in religious matters is a natural process with adolescent, yet it does not mean that an adolescent loses faith in religious matters without exception. The reasons for this doubt are but natural, because the base of doubts are the things about religious matters told to him during childhood and which now he judges according to his developed reasoning power and wider experience. The education particularly of subjects related to science are also a major factor in the creation of religious doubts. He not only entertains doubt about religious matters, but includes a wider range of subjects like family and social relationships, morality, sex and many other prevailing traditions and views. If the adolescent gathers courage, to go against the conventions, the elders raise a hue and cry and condemn his actions vehemently. This act is regarded as unjust by the adolescent. Psychologically an adolescent's doubts are not harmful to his future development. We have already said that adolescence is a revolutionary stage in an individual's life and as a result of this revolutionary change, he develops a new personality and analyses all problems of life from his own angle. Entertaining doubts means that he possesses his own personality and he is making an effort to shape his future life successfully. Those adolescents who do not entertain doubts may possibly not possess intelligence enough to critically examine. Views and actions coming before them. We may, therefore, safely conclude that entertainment of doubts is a healthy sign and those elders who disapprove of this feature are unjust and unreasonable. Instead of expressing resentment or anger, the elders should psychologically explain those things about which the adolescents entertain doubts.

Some Kinds of Religious Doubts

There are many types of doubts entertained by adolescents and their intensity or depth varies according to their mental developments. The various subjects of doubt may include idol-worship, nature and man, hell and heaven, rebirth, fate, belief in the existence of God, shape of God, what happens after death, various philosophies of life.

We shall now discuss certain things pertaining to religious development during adolescence :

Childhood Religious Education

Elderly people do not attach any importance to the religious queries of children and they tell them things about religious matters in a very casual way. For instance, a child is generally told that temples, churches, mosques and such other buildings are the houses where people offer prayers to God. They will not explain to children the religious implications of the same. The child will at that time believe the elders but when he starts developing further reasoning power, he analyses critically what he was told during childhood and because facts were not explained to him in a satisfactory manner, he naturally starts entertaining doubts. This situation may be avoided to a great extent if liberal religious education is imparted to children.

School Education

Education makes one broad-minded, liberal and reasonable. Through education he also develops reasoning power and comes to know many new things. Education of subjects dealing with sciences inspires him to find out causes and effects of a phenomenon. This breaks many old images and he loses faith in many previous beliefs. He starts analysing what he knows and what he learns. In this process he meets many frustrations, because he finds many things in which he had blind faith, earlier. This creates in his mind doubts relating to many religious beliefs. The prevailing education system and the teachers also help in creating doubts about religious beliefs. Consequently, the adolescent loses faith in many earlier beliefs, amends many of his religious views and strictly adheres to those which he thinks as proper and reasonable.

Free Reasons-based Views

We have already mentioned earlier at many places that during adolescent the reasoning power of an individual develops rapidly and he freely analyses many problems he comes across during his life. He is also inspired by his elders and teachers in this effort. Consequently he finds that religious beliefs and problems of practical life do not run on the same lines. This creates doubts in his mind towards his earlier religious views and he develops a very cautious approach towards new religious education.

During adolescence an individual comes in contact with many other individuals belonging to different religions. He comes to know many salient features of other religions and occasionally discusses them with his friends. This also creates doubts in some of his religious beliefs. So he tries to find out which religious beliefs are sound and worth following.

Immoral Acts of Some so-called Religious Persons

When an adolescent comes to know of immoral acts of such persons who are considered religious persons by the society he not only develops hatred for those persons, but also towards the religious beliefs they follow. This creates doubts in his mind.

Individual Differences in Religious Doubts

Individual differences in the nature of religious beliefs are present in adolescents. The intensity and duration also differs in them. Religious doubts among the people belonging to bigger towns and larger society are more common as compared to those living in smaller towns and smaller societies. This is because there is more adequate education in the bigger places and also opportunities for exchange of religious views.

IMPACT OF RELIGIOUS DOUBTS

Cropping up of religious doubts seriously affect the religious views of an individual. His devotion towards religion declines and he disbelieves many religious faiths for some time considering them as false. He does not attaches any importance to religious matters and devotes little time to such things. He gives up prayer and stops worshipping at religious places. As a result, he shows indifference towards spiritual values.

SOLUTION OF RELIGIOUS DOUBTS

An adolescent's religious doubts should be approached with a sympathetic attitude and under no circumstances these doubts should be suppressed because by so doing the adolescents emotional instability and restlessness will be increased. The adolescent should be given full opportunity to express his views frankly and discuss them with others. He will then realise that he is not the only person who faces such doubts. This will give him mental peace because he will know that there are others, too, who are with him in the same boat. Besides, he should also be given religious education according to his mental development keeping in view that his religious hunger is different to that of children. He should, therefore, be acquainted with liberal religious views after enlightening him on the blind-faiths of his childhood.

Emotional Intensity along with Religious Doubts

We know that adolescence is a period of intense emotional tension and religious consciousness. At this stage the individual's religious problems need solution and if others indulge in condemning and criticising him his emotional tension further aggravates submerging him in gloominess. He occasionally may lose his mental balance in such a condition and think of committing suicide. He may also show contempt and anger towards those persons who had taught him some religious things during childhood.

Love and Sympathy Necessary for Reconstruction of Religious Beliefs

Every individual needs some kind of religious beliefs in his life and an adolescent is not an exception to this. This need of some religious beliefs is more keenly felt during middle adolescence, because by then the individual wants to build his own principle of life. In building this principle, he expects help from religion, despite his religious doubts. He takes some time in developing faith and confidence in religion, because it is but natural that return of faith after doubt takes its time. He cools down when he finds all elderly persons condemning his apathy towards religions. He then realises that he cannot command social trust and respect by showing apathy towards religion. However, sometimes he also takes an extreme step and turns an atheist. Love and sympathy are, therefore, absolutely necessary in reconstructing religious beliefs in adolescents.

SUMMARY

Everyone needs some religious beliefs in life and an adolescent is no exception. Although there are no reliable methods to measure the religious aptitude yet some methods are employed to understand it. They include introspective report, retrospective report, objective test, diary and questionnaire method. It is better to employ more than one of these methods for obtaining reliable results.

An adolescent needs some religious beliefs and principles for mental peace. Unlike in childhood he does not blindly believes in religious matters and examines them critically on rational grounds. This reasoning creates in him many religious doubts and although he does not become irreligious, yet his faith in religious matters taught during early childhood is badly shaken. Study of science and other subjects, contact with followers of other religions, immoral acts of some so-called religious persons also help in the creation of religious doubts.

The impact of religious doubts is serious. Due to religious doubts the adolescent stops prayer and visit to worship-places. He becomes indifferent towards religious matters. He considers the earthly pleasures as supreme.

It is not wise to suppress religious doubts in adolescents. A liberal, broad-minded and sympathetic attitude towards adolescents is necessary for the reconstruction of religious beliefs in him. He should be enlightened with love on religious matters.

Exercises

1. Discuss the suitability of the various methods of study of religious life of adolescents.
2. Explain the nature of religious doubts during adolescence.
3. Explain the differences in the religious beliefs of young children and those of adolescents.
4. What are the causes of religious doubts during adolescence ?
5. Discuss the factors concerning religious development during adolescence.
6. How should we meet the religious doubts of our adolescents ?

Notes

1. By the author *Bal Manovigyan,* Chapt. XII, Ramnarain Lal, Allahabad, 1950.
2. Hollingworth, L.S. 'The Adolescent Child'. In Murckison, C., *Handbook of Child Psychology*, 2nd Ed. Revised, Worcester, Mass, Clark University Press, pp. 882–908, 1933.

13

Morality in Adolescents

Expectations from Adolescents

People have great expectations from adolescents. Responsible behaviours are expected of an adolescent by the society, whereas nobody expects the same from children. On the other hand older people laugh out and enjoy the misdeeds of children and readily forgive them. The adolescents are not extended guidance on all occasions. They have to apply their discretion in arriving at decisions in many matters. They should also know the moral standard of the society and act accordingly. An adolescent will not get the protection of parents if he acts against some social standards. The irresponsible acts of adolescents are mostly due to lack of proper environment and earlier opportunities not given to them to act independently. If the feelings of self-confidence, self-dependence and courage are instilled in them there is no reason why they will not handle a given situation confidently without committing errors of judgment.

Psychological Definition of Morality

Morality has no separate entity away from the society and the individual. Psychologists and idealists have different views about morality. The idealists think that a man is the same all over the world and human morality and values are the same everywhere, they believe that standards of morality apply equally to all men, nations and societies. The view of idealists based on the universality of human nature academically appears to be sound on the surface but the psychologists differ. A psychologist find different standards of morality prevailing in different societies. They, too, appear to be correct in their approach to a certain extent. They relate morality to the behaviour of the people. Traditions, culture and behaviour of men of one society differ from those of others. It is, therefore, not correct to compare the standards of one country with those of another. Various countries have developed their moral standards and values in different ways. Moral standards cannot, therefore, be claimed as lasting and universal. Different societies have developed different moral values for guarding their own self-interests. Therefore, a man has to abide by the moral values developed in his society. Any of his acts which hurts the interests of the society will be naturally considered immoral. One has a duty in such circumstances not only to protect the moral standard and abide by them, but also to make his own contributions towards the further development of the same. How one should act morally is not within the purview of this book. We shall deal here only with the development of morality in adolescents.

The Impact of Heredity

An adolescent is born in a society which already possess certain moral standards and values, so he is expected to abide by the same. Heredity plays an important role in making one follow the moral values already laid down by the society. The environment also influences one's behaviour in this respect. Heredity plays a vital role in determining one's level of intelligence and capacity to cope with certain moral standards. It is generally seen that the situation is most unsatisfactory among morons in this respect. Terman reached this conclusion on the basis of his researches. He found children with higher I.Q. fared 85% better than those whose I.Q. was lower. It has also been observed that morons abound amongst criminals. They fail to appreciate moral values in many situations and commit to crimes. The reason is probably that they come from poor and unhealthy environment.

Effect of Environment

Environment influences one's moral development to a large extent and we may safely say that one is a product of his heredity and environment. If the environment of the home is unhealthy, the moral development will not be satisfactory. In such an environment the seeds of crime find a fertile soil. As the child grows he comes out of the precincts of the house and passes most of his time with his friends. Naturally, the friend-circle becomes more important as compared to the family circle and starts influencing the moral developments of the child. Now if his friends are morally developed the individual will also be inclined to appreciate moral values, but in case the friends are morally depraved and corrupt, there is every likelihood that the individual may also indulge in immoral acts. Next, comes the society and things related to the adolescent. The adolescent, like others, constantly comes in contact with many kind of persons and things. Good company, healthy books, religious and moral education in schools, good films etc., help considerably good moral development of an adolescent. In short, we may say that physical development does not mean moral development. Moral development depends upon healthy environment sharp intelligence and keen interest in following moral values.

Attention on Psychological Moment in the Development of Morality

Development of morality is a gradual process. It develops in stages. This child after coming in contact with members of his family gradually learns what things are considered moral by them and what they discard as immoral. He also learns from the appreciations and denunciations of his acts by others. Similarly, when he goes to school, he learns what the teachers and his own companions consider moral and what they denounce as immoral. In company of his society he learns the same thing. It is, therefore, advisable to take care of the child since childhood and teach him moral things. Delay in this work or indifference will create difficulties, because it is difficult to reform one if he goes astray. Morality should be taught to children according to their mental development and at moments when he is psychologically prepared to accept the advice. The importance of psychological moment has been well emphasised by Montessori. If children are taught morality every now and then, they are likely to react adversely. This will be harmful to them, because it will develop a feeling of inferiority complex and they will start thinking that they are good for nothing.

Influence of Companions

During adolescence when children come out of their home circle, it is the influence of their companions which plays a vital role in developing their concept of morality. They pass more time in the company of friends and seeks their advice. They are frank with them and, therefore, discuss with them what he is taught at home. They try to scrutinise and evaluate matters relating to morality practised in their homes. When they find the two views — one of their family and another of their friends — dissimilar or conflicting. As a result, they develop worry and being more under the influence of their friends start flouting the parents' advice. They readily accept the views of friends. This sometimes develops in them a feeling of revolt against the elderly members of the family. This is so because the friends wield greater influence over them.

Opportunity for Deliberations

As the child grows his thinking and reasoning also develops. He is now not willing to accept advice without weighing them on rational grounds. He wants to stand on his own and develops his personality in his own manner. He tries to think about his future and plan it too. He wants to assert his personality more and more and develops morality on his own ideas. He scrutinises moral and immoral acts of the society and passes his own judgment. He wants to exchange views with the members of his family also, but, of course, he does not want to be dictated by them. It is, therefore, proper and psychologically correct to give him opportunities to discuss his views and exchange ideas. He should be convinced with arguments and not made to follow others' views on dictatorial terms.

Setting too High a Goal Harmful

Setting too high goals without taking into account one's own capabilities is very harmful. Such an idealist faces failure because he cannot achieve the goal in the absence of capabilities. He gets frustrated and develops a sense of inferiority complex. The adolescent comes in contact with people of different nature. These persons do not have the same standard of morality. This creates a complex problems before the adolescent who does not know whom to follow. His problem and mental restlessness increases a great deal when he finds even his parents and other elderly persons whom he respects do not observe those standards of morality which they preach to him. This comes to him as a great emotional shock. He loses respect for and confidence in his parents and elderly persons. He is overtaken by a strong feeling of revolt. He starts detesting them and becomes their bitter critic. His criticism is based on his own concept of morality, ideals and principles. He also now desires that others should follow his ideals and principles, and when he finds others not following him, he is disappointed. He also feels ashamed if he finds himself deviating or falling down from his own ideals. The basis of an adolescents' ideals may be traced to the training and teachings he receives during childhood. If during childhood efforts are made to make him an idealist without taking into account his capabilities the results may be disastrous later in life.

Result of Childhood Control

Parent's and guardians' control over children should be a judicious blending of liberal and strict control. If one during childhood is subjected to strict control, he may develop a feeling of revolt during adolescence. He starts finding faults with the rules and regulations made by elders and, therefore, he tries to flout them. He starts formulating his own rules and regulations and tries to live upto them. These rules and regulations are sometimes very hard and sometimes very flexible and are based on his reactions towards his childhood environment. If he thinks that the principles according to which his parents acted were too liberal, then he lays down stricter principles, for himself, and if he considers his parents' principles too hard his approach towards his principles may be then liberal.

Changes in Moral Principles due to Social Contacts

There is a difference between the family circle and outside environment. When the child comes out of the home circle, he finds the environment changed and faces some difficulty in adjustment. Similarly, when he goes from a smaller to a bigger school or from one society to another, he finds a changed environment and faces some difficulty in the necessary adjustment. On coming in contact with the society he has to change and adjust his behaviour in relation to that society.

Adolescent More Careful towards Others' Reactions

An adolescent has a greater regard for others' feelings and ideas as compared to child. For example, an adolescent in order to respect another person's sentiment may resort to lying and consider it proper.

The child will not care for that even if the other person happens to be his father. The child will not hesitate in calling a spade a spade without caring whether his so doing will embarrass or land his father into trouble. An adolescent may be careful and consider lying on such an occasion a virtue and a moral act.

Double Standard of Morality for Boys and Girls

In India the society is guilty of using double standards of morality for girls and boys. Some actions of girls which are considered immoral or disgraceful for them are not considered immoral for boys. For example, smoking, going to pictures or markets alone, laughing in public places or markets or running on roads are considered disgraceful or immoral for girls, but this standard does not equally apply to boys. This develops a sense of inferiority complex in girls and they develop some emotional tension.

Opportunity to Show Moral Behaviour

Many immoral behaviours on the part of children are not considered immoral and these are overlooked, because it is presumed that they did so due to ignorance. This is not the case with adolescents who are expected to distinguish between moral and immoral behaviour. However, this does not mean that possessing the knowledge of moral behaviour guarantees practice of the same. Had it been so, learned and so-called wise men would have never committed immoral acts. A man after acquiring knowledge of morality must get opportunity to practise them in difficult situations. It is also seen that a man indulges in immoral behaviours because of lack of confidence or faith in them. He also may commit immoral acts simply to attract others attention or for self-exhibition.

Rise of Discretion in Adolescents

During the early years it is the fear that makes the child to observe morality. It is not any feeling of repentance that makes him to observe moral standards. He at this stage fears punishment for immoral behaviours. The desire to get reward also inspires him to observe the code of morality. This condition generally continues upto childhood. His behaviours are not guided by discretion till this stage. They are mostly influenced either because of fear of punishment or because of the desire to get appreciation and reward. Discretion makes its appearance gradually when he enters the threshold of adolescence. He now develops the sense of shame and repentance on finding himself committing something wrong. If such situations are repeated frequently, he becomes dejected and leads an unhappy life. He may develop inferiority complex and indulge in day-dreaming and keep aloof from realities of life.

Control and Courteous Behaviour

Some sort of control over adolescents is necessary in the interest of proper development of morality, but unfortunately many parents fail to appreciate the distinction between the control exercised over the child and that over the adolescent. Many people out of tender feeling or sentiments do not see any difference between childhood and adolescence. They consider their adolescent children still small children and try to be very strict with them. This is wrong. There are also some other types of people who do not favour any control over adolescents. They think that adolescents are competent enough to know their interests and take decisions accordingly. They forget that wisdom comes after experiences and the adolescents do not have many experiences. So they cannot take stock of any situation and take correct decisions. Therefore some sort of control and guidance is necessary for adolescents. He should be educated in moral standards and values. Some punishments should also be there for delinquents. But what is more important is that while making provision for punishment, the state of development and the situation should be also taken into consideration. An adolescent, too, has a strong desire for appreciation of his conduct. He also wants recognition of his good work from the society. So he should be given ample scope to prove his merit and as regards punishments instead of corporal punishment, snubbing, rebuking, denying privileges and calling for explanation will suffice in most of the cases.

Corporal punishment is not advisable at any stage for an adolescent. However, there are many parents who are haughty and unpsychological enough to lose their temper and give corporal punishment to adolescents. This type of punishment results into terrible consequences. The adolescent may flout orders, destroy things, run away from home or stop talking with family members. He is filled with a feeling of vengeance because he feels that giving him corporal punishment was an unwarranted and unjust step. He tries to bring in disrepute his punisher and creates a gulf between his relationships. This gulf will not be created if the adolescent is convinced that the punishment awarded to him has been just. Many adolescents turn hardened criminals when they get unwarranted and unjust corporal punishments.

Tendency towards Committing of Crimes in Adolescents

Wrong education during childhood and a desire of self-exhibition often takes an adolescent towards crime and immoral behaviour. This feeling of self-exhibition is very strong during early adolescence and it diminishes gradually. He loses considerably this desire by the time he enters into mid-adolescence and in the last stage he develops a desire to abide by the moral code of the society. However, the impact of bad early education and bad society and environment may lead him towards committing crimes and during adolescence this tendency may reach the climax. The adolescent may due to this tendency resort to lying, stealing, running away from home, prostitution, smoking, drinking, sex-crimes, suicide, murder and smuggling etc. Evidently bad company, and bad education lead an adolescent towards immorality. Criminals are not born. It is the society and bad training which makes one criminal.

Root Causes of Crimes

Morons

The studies conducted by Healy, Rogers, and Austin prove that morons are more liable to take the path of crimes as compared to intelligent persons.

Unhealthy Environment

Unhealthy environment leads to criminal activities. One's atmosphere largely depends upon his social and economic status of the family. If the atmosphere in the family is bad, the child does not get an opportunity of good and healthy entertainment. This gives rise to unhealthy tendencies. Such children instead of passing their time in their homes go to their friends or places of vices which abound everywhere. They find their home-life miserable. So in such conditions they turn towards immoral behaviours just for a change.

Bād Family Condition

The quarrels between parents, their unpsychological behaviour and bad moral character often lead adolescents towards immorality.

Poverty

Poverty may be a breeding ground of many vices. Poor parents do not get enough time to look after their children. They are all the time engaged in solving their financial difficulties and are unable to extent affectionate behaviour towards children. Such children get uncontrolled and slip into vices.

Lack of Knowledge of Moral Principles

Due to incomplete or bad education some adolescents have no knowledge of virtues and vices. They are unable to distinguish between a moral and an immoral behaviour. Consequently, in utter ignorance they commit immoral behaviour.

Impact of Companions

Some adolescents sometimes commit immoral behaviour in order to rise in the estimate of their companions.

Inspired Acts

Some inspiration at times acts as an agent to vice. A tendency towards committing immoral behaviour may be present in some form or other in many persons, but this tendency remains inactive till there comes some stimulating factor. If a person remains away from the stimulating factor or is able to subdue it, he may be saved from vices, but when the environmental and stimulating factors combine together the adolescent may fall an easy prey to vices and his moral degeneration may start. The stimulating factor includes such causes as unhappy home life, influence of means of entertainment, sexual urge, undesirable flims, desire to get rich quickly, lethargy, obscene novels, unhealthy company etc. Sometimes subduing the natural instincts turns the adolescent towards immoral behaviour. Similarly, the desire of self-exhibition may become uncontrollable in an adolescent and he may commit immoral behaviour just to satisfy his desire. This is so because by subduing natural stimulations they find it difficult to indulge into self-exhibition in a natural and proper manner.

Punishment to Reform Adolescent

The real aim of punishment should be to reform the punished concerned. Since the dawn of civilisation till recently corporal punishment has been considered an effective measure to reform the erring individual. Some people consider corporal punishment as a panacea to reform guilty persons. Recent researches have proved that the proverb 'Spare the rod and spoil the child' is wrong and does more harm than good. Corporal punishment produces violent reactions in the mind of the adolescent. He revolts, becomes shameless and takes to vices more frequently. After a few repetitions of corporal punishment he gets used to it and remains unaffected. However, it is true that corporal punishment cannot reform, yet it is necessary in some cases to a certain extent. The corporal punishment is effective to a degree during childhood only, but if adolescents are subjected to such a treatment, it will simply amount to turning them into criminals. Corporal punishment inspires the feeling of vengeance against the person who inflicts the punishment. There is no dearth of such instances of adolescents turning into hardened criminals simply because of being awarded corporal punishments at times. Such adolescents get full of vengeance and defiant and arrogantly flout orders. This tendency causes indiscipline in future. The parents should, therefore, be very careful in awarding corporal punishment to adolescents. They should punish the adolescent only with the intention of reforming him, and if corporal punishment does not yield the desired result it should immediately be discarded at the first indication of failure. In some Western countries, besides reforming the adolescent, efforts are also made to reform the parents so that they may adopt more proper and psychological behaviour towards their children and not lead them towards crime by their unpsychological behaviour. In some countries, it is the parents who are punished with the intention of reforming them along with the child. Psychologists plead that punishment should be given only with a view to reform the delinquent. They should be properly educated regarding morality and immorality so that they behave correctly in a particular situation.

SUMMARY

People expect from adolescents that they are in a position to judge and shape their behaviour according to code of morality. They are not prepared to excuse them for their lapses as in the case of younger children. The concept of morality is not universal. The standards of morality changes from one society to another. Heredity also influences morality. Children coming from socially and economically better families observe more morality in their conduct. Environment vitally influences moral conduct of an adolescent. Morality should not be preached to the adolescent day in and day out. One should wait for the correct psychological moment to explain moral values.

Those adolescents who are idealists and set ambitious goal in life without taking into account their capabilities get frustration in return and develop inferiority complex. Very strict control during childhood proves harmful to children. Adolescents have to make some compromises in their moral principles when they come in wider contact of the society.

No one is a born criminal or immoral, and education alone does not make a man moral. One should get opportunities to practise moral behaviour.

Punishment should be given with the object of reforming the delinquent. Corporal punishment to a degree may be good for children but should be discarded in case of adolescents. It is harmful and it creates a feeling of revolt and vengeance and tends to make the adolescent shameless and criminal. The root causes of adolescents turning delinquents are lack of intelligence, unhealthy environment, poverty, bad and unpeaceful atmosphere of the home, ignorance of moral code and unhealthy effect of friends.

Exercises

1. Explain the factors that influence the development of morality in adolescents.
2. What is the role of environment in the development of morality in adolescents?
3. Why do some adolescents become immoral? Explain.
4. What are the root causes of immorality in adolescents ?

14

The Personality of Adolescents

WHAT IS PERSONALITY

Every human being whether a child, an adolescent or an adult possesses his own individual personality. This personality is reflected in all his activities and differs from individual to individual. The personality covers a wide range of traits and peculiarities of a person. It is very difficult to define personality in a few words, because of the wide area of human actions and reactions virtues and vices, capacity and incapacity it covers. Some people define the physical appearance of a human being as his personality. A handsome person according to them possesses a good personality. It is misleading. It is also equally wrong to say that an intelligent person has a good personality. All such definitions are one-sided. Actually speaking, the personality stands for the entire physical and mental development, character, conduct, behaviour, capabilities and ability for using discretion judiciously. It means that it is reflected in the coordination of all the human activities of an individual.

Personality compared with Sound

It will be easy to understand the meaning of personality if we compare it with sound. Just as it is difficult to see or touch some sound, in the same way you may feel the personality but you cannot see or touch it. We may feel personality and feel its impact, but cannot describe it adequately. In the case of sound at least two things are required — one producing it and the other hearing it. If there is none to hear it the sound has no significance. No body cares for sound produced in forests or deserted places. Similarly, in the case of personality there should be someone to see the personality of an individual. If there is no reaction in a person who sees an individual, then it is not a good or impressive personality.

Personality an Stimulating Power

Personality has one important trait. It causes reaction in others. The personality of a person may be charming to A, but repulsive to B, dominating to C, but submissive for D. This clearly means that it creates different reactions in different peoples. In other words, it stimulates others in one way or the other. This stimulating power is due to a person's coming into contact with different kinds of environments, things and persons. These contacts generate many reactions. The sum total of these reactions is the stimulating factor of one's personality.

Personality : Painting and Poetry

In order to understand personality in a more adequate manner, we may compare it with painting or poetry. Just as painting is not a combination of too many colours, or poetry not a combination of many words, but there is something deep in them to understand. Similarly, personality is not merely a combination of many traits, characteristics or reactions. There is in it some deeper meaning to understand. This some thing more is for a person to understand. It is difficult to define this 'something more'. Similarly, we cannot define poetry or painting clearly. We can only try to explain it. Different persons describe one's personality in different terms and with different angles. The personality covers a wide range of factors. These may be education, habits, moral character, temperament, physical appearance, wisdom, emotions, knowledge, ideals, objects, social approach, religious faith etc.

Factors Influencing Development of Personality

There are many factors that influence the development of personality. These factors are heredity, social and economic position, childhood experiences and other past experiences.

Impact of Heredity

There are divergent views about the impact of heredity on the development of personality. Some people are of the opinion that it has no influence, others hold that heredity definitely influences the development of personality. An individual's behaviour is influenced by his family environment. But is an individual the sole product of environment? Does he not acquire good and bad traits by virtue of his particular heredity reacting differently to the various environmental stimuli? Truly speaking, he acquires many such traits hereditarily and his personality is patterned according to an appreciable extent. Thus personality development is influenced both by environment and heredity.

Impact of Social and Economic Conditions

The influence of social and economic condition on development of personality cannot be denied. In hard pecuniary conditions it is difficult to get properly educated. If a person is not enjoying a good social position many evils may develop in his character. A socially and economically poor person is liable to develop inferiority complex, cowardice, lethargy and other bad habits.

Roots of Personality lie during Childhood

The personality of a person takes root during childhood and develops gradually. The experiences gained during childhood leave a permanent impact on the child's mind. The child's personality develops as he grows. Children who are brought up under a harsh discipline and whose natural aspirations are crushed in the name of discipline develop inferiority complex and get timid. They develop some other evils also. Similarly, those children who are pampered become haughty and lazy. Such children do not develop a healthy personality. Intelligent children easily gather knowledge and this factor helps in a good development of personality. The personality of intelligent children develop in a normal and healthy manner. Similarly, the children who are morons do not have a healthy personality. The personality of a child also changes during adolescence like other changes in him. His habits change, friends change, society and occupations change. This is because his environment changes and environment in his case means new schools, new teachers, new education, new friends and new attitude of guardians. All these factors influence the development on his personality because these have a tremendous impact on his mind. This impact either on the right or wrong side depends largely on the nature of the environment and physical development. Besides, impacts of childhood also influence the development of a person's personality. According to H.N. Gray the child learns some such habits which have both good and bad effect on others. The personality according to him is the result of his standard of living and behaviour. It (personality) goes on developing and taking a definite shape. By the age of ten years the outlines of one's future personality gets defined.

Impact of Past Experiences

C.K.A. Wang has conducted researches on the impact of past experiences on the development of one's personality. He has concluded that some aspects of a person's personality bears the impact of his childhood experiences. According to him snobbery may be found in a child who reads for the sake of fun and who takes much part in games. Timidity comes when the child finds few friends and devotes less time in studies. Introversion overtakes a child when he has few friends, few games and fewer opportunities for social entertainments. Plenty of friends and appreciation develop in the child extroversion, and taking too much interest in religious matters makes the individual's personality emotional. However, this does not mean that no changes are possible in future because of these factors. We have already stated in earlier pages that as the child advances in age his various faculties develop and he particularly develops a strong desire for getting recognition from others. In order to fulfil this desire, he is prepared to discard those habits which stand in his way. He does succeed in his efforts upto some extent and this means a change in his personality. However, childhood experiences play a vital role in shaping his personality. Researches made by Stanger show that children who pass childhood in misery develop a tendency to get emotional during adolescence. Shy children develop a feeling or habit of remaining aloof. This is also the case with children developing inferiority complex.

Some children become obedient and some adopt authoritarian attitude during adolescence. According to McLaughlin the reasons for developing these tendencies are as under :

Causes for Developing Traits of Disobedience

1. Unpsychological control of parents.
2. Lack of opportunities to handle responsible assignments.

3. Some physical deformity.
4. Trying to compare with elders.
5. Emotional difficulties during childhood and adolescence.
6. Contempt shown by classmates.
7. Sex shyness.

Causes for Developing Authoritarian Attitude

1. Handling responsible jobs early in life.
2. Teaching of self-confidence by the parents.
3. Frequent opportunities for social get-together.
4. Receiving pampering treatment from members of the family due to weak health.
5. Good at games and sports.
6. Good discipline at home.
7. Good physical and mental development.
8. Some good quality as a compensation to some defects.

Attractive Personality

In the foregoing pages it has been repeatedly stressed that there is a natural urge in adolescents to get recognition and appreciation from the society. Under the influence of this dominating urge he tries to keep away from such deeds as are condemned by the society. He also, side by side, tries to know which qualities are appreciated by the society and which are disliked. The adolescent, accordingly, tries to improve his personality by shedding off such traits which are looked down upon by the society. But at this stage, he is confronted with the problem of distinguishing between good and bad deeds. He finds that people entertain different opinions about different things. An act which is appreciated by one group of persons is considered bad by another group. However, in every society there are certain things and qualities which are mostly recognised as good. The person who possesses these qualities have a better personality. In fact, the personality of an individual is evaluated by the degree upto which he possesses qualities that are generally recognised as good by the society. According to E.G. Fleming[1] that personality is considered sound which has good social adjustment and whose emotional reactions may be depended upon.

Now we shall deal below the factors that influence the development of an adolescent's personality.

FACTORS INFLUENCING THE DEVELOPMENT OF AN ADOLESCENT'S PERSONALITY

Health plays a vital part in the development of adolescent's personality. Weak physique and frequent illness produce bad effects. Frequent illness generally affects the development of personality. Such weaklings develop intolerance, selfishness and jealousy. They also get short-tempered. These bad qualities, if not amended in time become a permanent feature of an adolescent's make-up. Guetzkow and Bowman[2] have studied the effect of continuous partial fasting (malnutrition) on adolescent's personality. They have come to the conclusion that such adolescents mostly spend their time in thinking about food. Their minds are so much occupied with thinking about food, that they get very little time to think about other matters. The adolescent becomes unsocial, coward and short-tempered during the period of fasting. Hardy[3] has studied the effect of illness during childhood on the development of adolescents personality. His findings are that occasional illness during childhood does not adversely affect the development of an adolescent's personality. It, on the other hand, helps the development of a more healthy tendency towards his environment. Nursing and treatment during the period of illness influence the development of personality. Some parents bother too much about their children's illness and make mountain out of a mole hill, whereas some exercise full control over their emotions and do not attach undue importance to children's illness. These two different approaches of parents produce two different kind of results. The parents in the first category instil a feeling of helplessness in their children, whereas the parents of the second category help develop a feeling of self-dependence and self-confidence in their children. Illness during adolescence also affects the development of personality. Some children remain healthy throughout childhood but fall seriously ill during adolescence. They, consequently, develop a feeling of inferiority complex.

Built of Body

We have already remarked earlier that a pleasing personality is greeted with favourable reactions. The reactions after viewing a well built muscular person are different from the reactions experienced after seeing a short statured and disease-ridden individual. An individual is influenced by the reaction of other persons and consequently he tries to improve his behaviour and appearance. In previous chapters we have hinted that an adolescent is greatly concerned over the development of his body because his body undergoes a revolutionary change during this period. The physical development during adolescence brings a new change in the outlook towards life and also towards other people. The adolescent goes a step further and adopts a new outlook towards his own self. The society further contributes in the development of this new outlook[4]. The adolescent is very keen to know the reaction of others towards his speedy physical development and by coming in contact with others he soon knows what their expectations are from him. He tries to live upto the expectations of other persons although in so doing he often feels shyness, pride, frustrations and inspirations. The adolescent in his efforts has to remain constantly in a state of struggle. This struggle gives a new shape to his personality.

The following aspects of the personality are generally considered good and bad by others :

Unpleasing Aspects of Built and Appearance :

1. Extra-ordinary height or very short height.
2. Too fat or too lean.
3. Too dark or too fair complexion.
4. Indifferent health.
5. Physical weakness, weak eye sight or weak hearing power, long nose, thick lips, bulging out teeth.
5. Small eyes.
6. Ugly way of walking : trotting, bending; projecting chest, jerking shoulders or hands while walking.
7. Wearing too bright coloured clothes or dirty ones.
8. Putting on badly tailored garments.

Pleasing Aspects :

1. Average height — Neither too tall nor too short.
2. Good health.
3. Neither too fat nor too lean — Proportional in relation to height.
4. Physically powerful.

5. Good walking style.
6. Normal eye sight and hearing.
7. Good set of teeth.
8. Clean body and cleanly clothed. No artificial make-up like powder, cream etc.
9. Fair complexion. It should not be too dark.
10. Well tailored clothes.

The adolescent learns these things when he comes in contact with others and accordingly analyses his personality. As a result of this analysis he tries to adopt such manners which are appreciated by the society. This gives a new outlook to his personality.

REACTION TOWARDS THE NAME

Effect on Personality

Generally the elder members of the family do not realise the significance of a name in relation to personality. They sometimes name a child according to their own outdated notions. The effects of name on the personality is of far-reaching importance and it is difficult to escape from it. Ugly names are often responsible for inferiority complex or failures. Of course, this does not mean that men with attractive names are always successful in life. However, the influence of the name on the personality is vital, because pleasing names help generate self confidence in a man whereas ugly names adversely affect the growth of the same.[5]

Impact of Names

There is a general tendency to name the children after the heroes and great men of the country. In India people honour characters mentioned in the *Puranas* or mythological stories or epics. They love them and therefore name their children after them. We do not find children bearing the name of villains. The reason is self-explanatory. People do not want their children to follow the example of infamous characters. They want their children to follow the footsteps of great men after whom they have been named. Similarly, nicknames also indicate special qualities. Nicknames are given after the qualities possessed by an individual. Healthy and brave children are given the nickname of Bhim or Sandow, gentle and meek children are nicknamed after a saint by their friends. Similarly, idiots are called 'Buddhu' and intriguers or back-biters are nicknamed accordingly.

SOCIAL RELATIONSHIP

We have already said that the influence of social relationship over the adolescent is quite remarkable. Now we shall discuss how different kind of social relationships influence the development of adolescent's personality.

Family

The personality of the adolescent is greatly influenced by the various members of the family. A tense family atmosphere produce emotional instability in the adolescent. Too much strictness by the parents create an urge of revolt in some adolescent and in some it develops an inferiority complex. On the basis of his researches L.H. Stott[6] has concluded that an adolescent may be made a fine social being through inspiration, good atmosphere and good guidance by the members of the family. Those homes where members quarrel with each other never help healthy development of adolescent's personality. Adolescents coming from such homes become haughty, quarrelsome and indifferent towards social recognition. They lack self-control and develop frustration. The bad influence or bad social and financial condition of a family over the adolescent has already been pointed out several times in preceding pages.

The Only Child

The effect of being the only child plays an important role in the development of one's personality. The reasons are many. Such a child is the centre of attraction of the entire family. Nobody wants to displease him. His wishes are mostly carried out. His mischief is tolerated. Even his bad traits are regarded as good points and his each act whether good or bad is applauded. All these affect the child's personality. This effect becomes more clear during adolescence. If he is given the same attention during adolescence he is likely to become haughty and may also lack the quality of self-dependence. However, it is the behaviour of persons surrounding the child and not the position of being the only child that affects the development of personality. If the only child is brought up on sound psychological principles, he may also develop a sound personality like other individuals.

Parental Control : Strict or Slack

Symonds in his book *Psychology of Parent Child Relationship* advocates strict parental control over children. In his opinion strict control develops good social outlook in children and creates interest in children towards studies. However, there is also a darker side of strict control. Strict control may also develop a sense of inferiority complex, emotional disturbance and lack of courage to express fearlessly. Slack control encourages the child to become obstinate. Such children may also lack a sense of responsibility. They turn naughty, do not pay attention towards studies, become indolent, develop dirty habits and create nuisance in their class rooms. However, they develop the virtue of fearless expression. The child brought up under strict control acquires the virtues of obedience, courtesy, vigilance, loyalty, honesty, self-sufficiency and self-confidence but he may also become timid. Children brought up under slack control may develop the bad traits of disobedience, obstinacy, haughtiness, high handedness and carelessness, but they may also develop such traits as self-confidence and independence. Anderson has observed that the children of parents who are too affectionate also develop the traits of cooperation, emotional stability, obedience and cheerfulness, but the children of parents exercising strict control acquire the bad traits of non-cooperation and quarrelsome spirit. Thus strict and slack control influence the development of an adolescent's character in its own way.

Impact of Parental Love over Children

Symonds in his book entitled *A Study of Parental Acceptance and Rejection*, has given conclusions of his researches on the impact of parental love on the personality of an adolescent who receives it or who is denied it. According to Symonds worry overtakes those children who are denied parental affection. They create nuisance in schools habitually and become back-benchers. They develop criminal tendencies. They become anti-social elements. Children who receive parental affection are generally social, emotionally stable and cooperative in outlook. The conclusion drawn by Symonds from his observations and studies is that adolescents who become good citizens, eminent scholars, good social workers, affectionate husband, wife or parents comes from families where parental love flows freely.

Copying an Ideal

An adolescent by nature is an idealist. So he tries to choose an ideal to develop his personality on that line. He tries his best to follow that ideal. He tries to find out a living ideal and then tries to copy him. Many adolescents accept his teacher as his ideal and try to adopt his modes of behaviour.

TWO TYPES OF PERSONALITY

Often it has come to light that some person's personality does not develop on the desired lines and some defects creep in. The root of the defects may be traced to their childhood. Some maladjustment during childhood result in future defects in personality. Unfortunately, little attention is given to this shortcoming during childhood. Personality, according to Strang[7], is of two types. The first category includes those whose behaviour is satisfactory for themselves and in the second category fall those whose behaviour is satisfactory for the society, but they themselves are victims of mental anguish. Those who do not try to solve their problems become fatalists in temperament. The defects which appear unimportant during childhood assume great dimensions during adolescence and it becomes a difficult task, to overcome them at this stage. Some undesirable traits in the development of personality are pointed out below :

Irresponsibility

Indolence is the root cause of irresponsible behaviour. When an individual sinks himself into indolence he starts neglecting his duties. Consequently, he becomes an irresponsible person. The environment plays an important part in the growth of this bad trait.

Excessive Enthusiasm

Excessive enthusiasm is born out of lack of self-confidence. Although an adolescent is keen to do a job and tries to tackle it with full enthusiasm, yet he finds himself in midst of chaos. He is unable to find his path and is in search of guidance but hesitates in seeking the same because he thinks that people will consider him immature. He, therefore, does not take advice from elders but instead approaches his friends or anyone whom he thinks his well-wisher.

Feeling of Doubt or Fear

Doubt is created when a person lacks self-confidence in his ability. Such a person always harbours a fear of committing mistakes and in removing this complex he tries to mould his behaviour according to the nearest society. By mid-adolescence this feeling nearly vanishes and the adolescent gets more composed. In case he does not get over this weakness, he develops many bad habits. It may be possible that he becomes too sensitive and intolerant towards others who offer him some advice. In order to escape from an advice he tries to do work in an extremely cautious manner.

Dislike to Go Out

Some adolescents avoid leaving home although they may not be very much attached towards the members of their family. In fact, they are shy of new environment. Their behaviour resembles children and they actually are dependent like children.

Indulging in Fantasies

Fantasies carry the adolescent away from realities of life. He creates for himself an imaginary world of his own. Although at some time or the other everyone enjoys some. fantasies, but adolescence is a period when an individual immerses in the sea of fantasies. Some adolescents remain too much under the influence of fantasies. This state adversely affects his personality, because he is away from practical experiences of life.

Regression

Regression is a result of an individual's incompetence and helplessness. He tries to give up his current behaviour and adopt an old behaviour. Regression is generally observed in an individual's social activities.

Rationalised Projection

An adolescent is keen on winning appreciation from others. In case of failure he tries to escape social condemnation by blaming others. He tries to give evidence in his efforts to put blame on others and thus derives false satisfaction. A victim of rationalised projection thinks that the entire society is against him and not he but others are responsible for his failure. Needless to remark that a rationalised projection is a glaring defect in an individual's personality.

The reader is advised to read some other relevant books for understanding the methods of measuring personality, as it falls beyond the purview of this book in hand.

Symptoms of Well adjusted and Mal-adjusted Personality

Adolescence is a period of great upheavals in one's life. So it is a period of great difficulty for the adolescent. He does not get mental peace till he adjusts himself in the environment. If the adolescent is fortunate to get good education, guidance and sympathy, he will gradually find solutions of problems facing him and be happy. The desires of well-adjusted and mal-adjusted are as under :

Desires of Adolescent with Well-adjusted Personality

1. To attempt welfare of the mankind.
2. To achieve outstanding success and fame in life.
3. To achieve highest degree of efficiency.
4. To make friendship with good persons.
5. To imbibe good qualities.
6. To keep engaged in important assignments.
7. To achieve peace.
8. To receive the best and higher education.

Desires of Adolescent with Mal-adjusted Personality

1. To earn money.
2. No labour in education. No attending of schools.
3. To keep engaged in entertainment.
4. Reading books without any good objective.
5. Undertaking journey without any definite prógramme.
6. Desire of ever-changing residence.
7. To procure some service.
8. Desire of having good luck and opportunity.
9. To be an opportunist.

It cannot be said definitely that the adolescents whether having a well-adjusted or mal-adjusted personality will act according to their desires, but certainly many of their actions will bear the impact of their inclination.

Happy and Unhappy Adolescents

Intelligence of a high order is not the sole element to make an adolescent's life happy. There are many other factors that bring happiness to people. The adolescent, in fact, gets real happiness by success in his work and pursuits. Some adolescents feel very happy by getting fame. Frustration in love affairs makes an adolescent unhappy. Some adolescents spoil their entire life, if they do not get life partners according to their fancies. Such adolescents find solace in music and poetry. Happily adjusted adolescent are not afraid of facing the realities of life. The mal-adjusted adolescent remains immersed into his own emotions and interests of his near relations. The happy adolescent succeeds in making his life an ideal and based on principles. The unhappy one is so much engrossed in various personal problems that he gets no time to plan a definite programme or choose an ideal. He may be compared to a rolling stone. He feels uneasy if he fails to improve himself. There is no cheerfulness on his face. He appears to carry the burden of the entire world on his shoulders. The author feels that most of the adolescents trying to become musicians and poets suffer from unhealthy feelings and frustrations and if they are not duly guided they will surely spoil their lives.

SUMMARY

Personality reflects the impact of the entire development of the individual. The modes of behaviour may be regarded as a mirror of one's personality. Personality includes all the good and bad traits that an individual possesses. It is through his behaviour that these good or bad traits are manifested. The development of personality is the result of interactions between hereditary and environmental factors. The development of personality is a continuous process. It starts from the very birth and goes upto the last breath of the individual. The varying experiences from the very consciousness of the individual contribute towards the development of his personality. Parental control, strict or otherwise, has to play a major role in the development of one's personality. Companions of adolescents are generally responsible for most of the good or bad traits of the personality of an adolescent. If the individual is not properly brought up, he develops many complexes. These complexes make him mal-adjusted in life in various ways.

Exercises

1. Discuss the nature of personality and explain the factors that contribute to its development during adolescence.
2. How do varying experiences contribute to the development of different traits of personality ? Explain with illustrations from an adolescent's life experiences.
3. Explain the factors that make an adolescent's personality attractive and pleasing.
4. Discuss the role of parents in the development of adolescent's personality.
5. How does an adolescent try to effect adjustment in his life in midst of various unpleasant experiences ? Explain with some concrete illustrations.

Notes

1. Fleming, E.G. *Pleasing Personality, J. Soc. Psychol.* 3, 100-107, 1932.
2. Guetzkow, H.S. and Bowman, P.H., *Man and Hunger*, Elgin II, Brethren Publishing House, 1946.
3. Hardy, M.C. "Adjustment Scores of Adolescents having a history of frequent illness during Childhood." Hmer, *J. Orthopsychiat*, 7, 204-209, 1937

4. Stoltz, H.R. and Stoltz, D.M. 'Adolescent Problems Related to Somatic Variations', 43rd. Years, *Nat. Soc. Stud. Educ.* pp. 80-99, 1944.
5. Hurlock, E.B., *Adolescent Development*, p. 473, McGraw-Hill Book Company, Inc., First Edition, New York, 1949.
6. Stott, L.H. 'Personality Development in Farm, Small Town and City Children', Univ. Nebar, Agric. Expert Station, Res. Bull. No. 114, 1939.
7. Strang, R. 'Guidance in Personality Development', 37th year, *Nat. Soc. Studies, Educ.* Part I, pp. 197-228, 193.

15

Adolescents Needing Due Guidance

Adolescents often talk about education and earning money amongst themselves. One will say 'I have no love for the school'. The other will reply 'I deeply love the school'. 'Even food is unimportant before studies'. Some one may comment 'Members of my family are fed up with my education'. An adolescent girl may remark 'What is the harm if I do not study? Are there no illiterate in the world passing their days? How happy they are'. 'I want to get a service and leave school'. 'I Love to roam about and do not like to study'. 'I want to help my father in business. I do not need much education'. Similarly, some adolescent may say 'I simply want to enjoy my life. Studies are boring to me' or 'No one has any regard for me in the house and everyone taunts at me' or someone may say, "Nothing interests me except the games".

The above words of adolescents clearly indicate that their tastes, interests and aptitudes vary. They entertain different views about schools, games and social activities. A few years earlier very little attention was paid towards the aptitude and various faculties of children. Those adolescents who were not interested in pursuing studies were allowed to give up the same. Then, the subjects of studies in schools were mostly compulsory. Very few subjects were optional. But the situation has changed after the attainment of independence in our country. Both the Government and the people have started now taking keen interest in education. So education is now available to everyone who desires to have it. Educationists have made researches and attention now is given to a student's aptitude. In foreign countries like USA, England, France, Germany etc. contents of studies are prepared taking into account the different aptitude of the students. In India, too, much activity is seen in the field of education. In many spheres researches and new experiments are being carried out and scope of studies is being enlarged. However, we should not lose sight of the fact that students not only differ in studies and intelligence but also in many things which mostly relate to their physical and mental capabilities. In such circumstances, it is desirable that educationists should seek the cooperation of psychologists in order to find out the various requirements of adolescents. If this is not done, it is possible that efforts put in for educating children may not give adequate results. The Central and the State Governments owe particular responsibility in this regard.

Necessary Enthusiasm and Inspiration

Adolescents are overzealous, idealist and fame-hungry, so it is desirable that these qualities are exploited for the sake of educating and reforming them and thus giving a new direction to their life. Unfortunately, many teachers lose sight of this important factor. The teachers must realise that physical and mental powers, although inter-dependent to a certain extent, are also independent of each other. Keeping this fact in view, one cannot foretell that failure in one field may also lead to failure in another. No doubt an adolescent with a keen intelligence may better fare in many areas. If he is encouraged, he may also go ahead in games and sports. Many adolescents do not understand the importance of self-confidence and determination. So the adolescents should be taught the importance of the same by parents and teachers. Success in life depends 99 per cent on perspiration and one per cent on inspiration. So at first, adolescents should be acquainted with their possibilities and then be inspired to achieve their goals of life.

Worry about Social Adjustment

Social adjustment is necessary for an adolescent and for this he must develop certain traits. The possession of these traits will enable him to perform his everyday work efficiently. Some persons feel that during adolescence a certain amount of slackness is visible over the physical equilibrium, activeness and adjustment of various other faculties. This state of affairs is very harmful because it is during adolescence that the adjustment of various faculties is needed most. The saving grace is that this slackness is only a temporary feature. So this slackness does not harm the adolescent's social adjustment much. The parents' duty is to keep a critical eye over the different social experiences of the adolescents in relation to their social impact.

Probably it is due to this reason that in advanced foreign countries social experiences are included in the contents of studies and teaching methods. Many researches, experiments and studies are being conducted in these countries to achieve better results. It is beyond the scope of this book to discuss these studies and experiments. However, the readers may consult relevant book for the same.

The adolescents, besides experiencing the physical and mental development, also experience many other things related to social development. Those persons who are concerned with the education of adolescents should pay attention to this aspect. This is a difficult job because the experiences of adolescents are varying. The pace of their development differs, their outlook, aptitudes, tastes, expectations and ambitions greatly differ. Almost all adolescents are consciously or unconsciously influenced by their social adjustment problems. Naturally the related anxiety is present in them. The reactions of teachers and adults towards adolescent's anxieties are generally as under :

1. Appreciation.
2. Contempt.
3. Anger over carelessness of adolescent.
4. Indifference towards his achievements.
5. Rejection of adolescent's demand for freedom.
6. Anger over adolescent's queries.
7. Feel flattered over adolescent's success.

This must be kept in mind that there is an intimate relationship between teacher's reactions over the activities of adolescents and their social adjustment. The teachers should, therefore, adopt a psychological approach in their behaviour and conversation with adolescents.

Teacher's Responsibility towards Social Development

Proper study of various subjects and learning a trade according to aptitude is very necessary for proper social adjustment for an adolescent. The social stature of the adolescent rises when he learns some fruitful practical art. Successful education now means successful social adjustment. So teachers' responsibility has been extended upto social adjustment of the adolescent. Possessing the spirit of forgiveness and discharging social responsibilities are indications of good social adjustment. The teacher's responsibility in this respect is so great that even very efficient teachers do not rise upto the expectations. Sometimes adolescents become totally dependent on teachers and obey teacher's order as if these are the dictates of God. Teachers have to avoid such a situation, because the adolescent in this condition will never acquire the quality of self-dependence and self-introspection which are very necessary for good social adjustment.

Offering Opportunity to Discharge One's Responsibilities on Democratic Lines

The adolescent wants some opportunity to discharge his responsibilities. He wants others' help in solving his problems. His happiness depends upon fulfilment of his needs. Very few persons in our country are able to continue study till the end of adolescence. Poverty compels many to leave school and earn money by joining some service or business. The adolescent's aptitude towards the work depends on his early education, social and financial standing and the environment around him. The adolescents who have to give up studies and join service expect the same sympathy and co-operation from those around him as he used to get in the school. Often their expectation remains unfulfilled, because they need proper social adjustment in the new environment. Moreover in the new environment, there are different types of people holding different views. For example, some demand more rights and some stand for personal freedom.

The adolescent's reactions towards various types of persons differ. They may show timidness and lack of initiative while working under an officer. They may become indisciplined when the supervision becomes slack. They may feel frustrated at their own behaviour. They may also show lack of understanding when allowed to work independently. In USA and U.K. the adolescent, when given an opportunity to act independently works with greater responsibility. His output is more satisfactory. Although we are also a democratic nation we have yet to develop aptitude, behaviour and actions in keeping with the democratic ideals. Today's adolescents are the future citizens and leaders of tomorrow. We have, therefore, to build up their character in such a manner that they become worthy citizens of a great democratic nation.

Adolescents Need Sympathetic Behaviour

Adolescents often face bitter experience while doing a work either in the home or outside. This is visible from their frustrated behaviour or indifferent attitude. However, if they are educated in a psychological and intelligent manner they may rise to dazzling heights. In adolescents, too, signs of cruelty, aimlessness and frustration as in the adults may be observed, but when they are offered a suitable opportunity, they may produce better results also. The adolescent should not be discouraged due to some failure. On the other hand, he should be told not to lose heart. He should be encouraged in all manners and offered help. This approach will yield wonderful results, because he will then go all out to achieve success.

How to Guide the Misguided Adolescents

There are three ways to guide a misguided adolescent: (1) To praise his good behaviour, (2) To modify the ideal before him, and (3) To encourage him to change his approach. Adolescents should not be given sermons on virtues, but should be offered opportunities to learn them. They should not be snubbed on mistakes. The teachers and parents must not lose sight of the fact that no man in the world is perfect. Somewhere and sometimes something is always wrong in each person. Cooperation should be sought from adolescents in activities in which they are interested. They will, in this way, feel honoured. They should also be entrusted with functions related to public responsibility. The parents and guardians should show affectionate behaviour and treat them like friends. They should not be treated as mere small children. The teachers should also do likewise in the schools.

Environment of Adolescent's Liking

In the sphere of learning the adolescent's desire is to learn the art of becoming self-dependent. He also desires to learn good qualities. These desires of adolescents are fulfilled only when the teacher, too, is emotionally and socially mature. The adolescent desires sympathetic treatment from the society. He wants opportunity for winning appreciation, performing courageous tasks and discharging responsibility to enable the society to recognise his work. He also wants adequate opportunity to learn arts, music, religion, literature and life's philosophy. He expects the society to offer him opportunity to accomplish all these pursuits. In service he expects courteous behaviour. He wants that whatever little he does should receive proper attention and not overlooked. In short, he desires a courteous behaviour from others and it is not impossible to extend him courtesy and sympathy. This will also not jeopardize the interests of adults and others concerned.

Contribution of Adolescents to Social Development

Society reflects the collective culture and has a tendency to change with time. It also represents the good features of past, because the present is the child of the past. Society is ever-changing because man is always going ahead, on the road of progress. The adolescents of today do not live in the same environment in which adolescents lived half a century ago. Their problems are now different and their approach to life, too, differs. With the progress of society the culture, too, undergoes a change, because culture does not mean stagnation. The adolescent should, therefore, be so guided that they may be able to contribute their best to make proper changes in the society.

The behaviour of adolescents is influenced by many things, but there are certain values and principles in the society which do not pay proper attention to adolescents' different personal traits. The result is that every adolescent projects for himself an imaginary world of his own for a short period and fulfils his desires in imagination. The duration of this imaginary world depends on the environment around him. It is desirable that the adolescent leaves this imaginary world and comes to the real world soon. This will help him to solve his real problems more satisfactorily.

Attention on Different Personal Behaviour

It is necessary to pay attention to an adolescent's individual characteristics while teaching him. The individual behaviours of adolescents differ and by paying particular attention to this aspect, many problems of adolescents may be automatically solved. The teacher has to select such parts of the text books which relate to differences in individual behaviour. After the selection is made the teaching method should be adjusted accordingly. The following points of view should be kept in mind while planning the curriculum :

1. Attention should be paid to different needs of adolescents.
2. Emphasis should be on co-operation and democratic principles and ideals.
3. Ample opportunity for researches and experiments should be provided.
4. Opportunity for self-expression should be adequately given.

Duty of Teachers

The adolescent wants to shower the love he received from his parents in childhood on others. At this stage of development he often falls victim to emotional instability. The teacher's responsibility increases manifold at this time. He, therefore, has to study very carefully the behaviour of the adolescent in all respects. The teacher represents the entire society in bringing an adjustment between the adolescent and the environment. The teacher faces a big difficulty in this task because he finds a relationship between the adolescent's stable and instable behaviours. He has to grasp this link and only then he can give the adolescent in a psychological manner. The secret is that the adolescent is more prone to listen to the teacher and act when emotionally instable. However, other things also count. There must be some such thing in the text-book, in the teacher's behaviour and other related activities which may fulfil his emotional requirements. The adolescent sometimes remains in an imaginary world. The teacher must bring him down to the real world. He should not be treated like a child or an adult.

Schools and persons connected with education and development of adolescents must bear in mind the following points :

1. Good social experience.
2. Taking part in neighbouring social activities.
3. Finding out the vocational aptitude and preparing the curriculum accordingly.
4. To offer such activities which may enable an adolescent to understand his responsibilities, personality and duties.
5. Encouraging him to consider his requirements and deal with his problems like an adult citizen and member of a family.
6. To encourage him to study the ideals and principles of his society and make effort to set ideal of a high order.

School Laboratory

The curriculum for the adolescent should be prepared keeping in view all the above points. The teacher should also realise his duties and position. No doubt the teacher cannot prepare a curriculum for each adolescent. However, if he guides and advises the student at the right moment it may become the turning points in the adolescents career. The teacher must not consider the adolescent as an adult with fully developed personality. The emotional instability should be considered a stage in the development of his personality. In the school, if these points are kept in mind, then it may serve as a laboratory for the development of an adolescent's personality. Each school should function as a laboratory of this nature.

SUMMARY

Quite naturally, adolescents have varying interests, aptitudes and abilities. Each one has his own notions regarding various things in the world. He is full of various ideas and lacks the necessary equilibrium. He needs sympathy and an attitude of understanding for himself on the part of others. He confronts varying problems of social adjustment. For this adjustment he is in need of other's appreciation of his points of view and difficulties. Teachers and elders in the family owe a special responsibility in this context. The adolescent wants that he should be adequately heard and his desires and wants should not be ignored. He wants that teachers and others concerned should behave on democratic lines. An attempt should be made to provide the necessary environment in order to enable him to effect the necessary adjustment in an acceptable and satisfying manner. The school should offer opportunities for various types of activities in order to meet the various legitimate urges of the adolescents. The place of the home cannot be ignored in this respect.

Exercises

1. What are the points that we should specially keep in mind in organising education of our adolescents ? Explain with some concrete illustrations.
2. How can we provide opportunities in the school and home for the necessary adjustment of adolescents ? Explain with some examples.

16

Adolescents and Maturity

Various aspects of maturity have been dealt with briefly in this chapter. The idea behind is that parents, and teachers may get an idea of their duties and responsibilities towards adolescents so that they may be able to give them the correct guidance. They have to get an idea of adolescent psychology. Only then they will be in a position to understand the problems and behaviours of adolescents. In the absence of this knowledge one fails to understand as to how he will be able to guide the adolescents. In the earlier pages we have already hinted at some of the points that the teachers and parents should bear in mind in the process of guiding adolescents.

DEFINITION OF MATURITY

As one grows mature his emotional stability and depth of social adjustment, vocational and professional aptitude, life's ambitions etc. go on developing[1]. A mature person is expected to understand a situation without anyone's help and realise his duties and responsibilities himself. He will not act in an irresponsible manner under emotional strain and waste his energy and time over imaginary problems.

Age Alone Not Related With Maturity

Age alone does not bring maturity to a person. Often people think that one becomes mature after he crosses the stage of adolescence, that is, after he attains the age of 21 or 22 years. However, it is to be kept in mind that it is not necessary that one's behaviour becomes mature with age. There arc numerous persons who despite age behave like children. They lack emotional stability. Often one may find some grown up persons who quarrel like children, throw away things, leave the house in anger or create disorder in the room. Many such persons may be found talking like children or dancing like small boys when happy. Such persons can never be happy in their life. On the other hand, they will produce emotional instability in those persons who are nearer to them and make their lives also unhappy. It is also a fact that no man is perfect and no one is perfectly mature. However, the greater degree of maturity one acquires, the greater service he renders to the society.

Relation of Maturity Development with other Stages

It is the mature person who counts in the modern society. The children, old persons and adolescents do not carry much weight in worldly matters. Many ideals and values for the society are set by mature adults. In fact, mature persons are the driving force behind the society. But this does not mean that children and adolescents are worthless and older people useless for the society. The children and adolescents of today are the mature persons of tomorrow. Therefore, they cannot be neglected. Similarly, the experience of old persons is valuable in guiding the mature adults. So they, too cannot be cast aside as useless. In short, children, adolescents, mature adults and old persons have their own importance in the society.

Impact of Modern Civilisation on Physical Maturity

Before reaching maturity an individual has to pass through many difficult stages in this age of modern civilisation. At the beginning of civilisation, that is, in the ancient period when civilisation was in its infancy the human being did not face so much difficulties. With the development of civilisation, on the one hand, man is becoming stronger in many aspects, but on the other hand, physical maturity in, many aspects is getting lower. When one has to put in hard labour to earn his bread, he does not face much difficulty in achieving physical maturity. But in the modern period many persons have not to put in much physical labour in winning their bread. Consequently, today we are much behind our forefathers in the sphere of physical maturity. This fact is supported by the findings of biologists and zoologists.

Desire and Non-Desire for Achieving Maturity

People think that the life of a child is a happy one because he is free from duties and responsibilities. They desire to become once again a child. Generally, when a person is posed with too many problems and he is worried he desires to go back to childhood. But if a child is asked about his life he will say that he is not happy with his life as a child. He, on the other hand, may say that he wants to become a mature adult and enjoy all those rights which a mature one enjoys. In fact, it is a secret of life that one thinks that the other one is happier. There are, of course, exceptions too. Many children want to remain children and similarly there are many mature adults who want to remain mature adults.

Maturity has both its brighter and darker sides. We shall hint at these sides briefly onwards.

Advantages of Maturity

Freedom

A mature adult enjoys freedom which is not available to children. The children have mostly to remain under the control of their parents.

Satisfaction

A mature adult derives satisfaction from his various abilities. He develops greater emotional stability. Children and adolescent have no correct idea about their capabilities. They generally indulge in making schemes. So they lack emotional stability.

Fearlessness

A mature man has greater courage in facing problems because during his development he learns many things through experiences. Children and adolescents are mostly afraid of committing mistakes.

Disadvantages of Maturity

Face the Consequences

The mature adult has to own the responsibility for his actions. The children and adolescent may escape from owning the same.

Alone in the World

A mature adult is virtually alone in the world. He is subjected to criticism occasionally. He cannot take shelter behind anyone like children or adolescents. The mature adult has to face difficult situations all alone and cannot expect help like children.

Some Types of Maturity

Physical Maturity

Physical development is a gradual process. No part of the body develops suddenly. It takes from 18 to 20 years for adequate physical development. It is not necessary that physical maturity is accompanied with emotional, social, mental and moral maturity. However, it is generally observed that as one grows he gains valuable experiences. Consequently, we may conclude that physical maturity is deeply related with emotional, social, mental and moral maturity.

Emotional Maturity

Children and adolescents do not have much emotional maturity because their control over their environment is not adequate. The mature adult due to development of his various powers has greater control over his environment. So he possesses emotional stability to a greater degree. The emotional maturity begins during adolescence. The adolescents differ in degree with each other in this development. We shall hint at the nature of maturity onwards.

Power to Bear Emotional Tension

An emotionally matured man has full control over the expression of his feelings. Those who are emotionally immature often speak and act in an irresponsible manner. No doubt there should be an outlet for the flow of emotional tension, otherwise the individual will continue to suffer mental tension. The emotionally mature persons, however, behave according to the accepted social values and ideals.

Indifference towards Emotional Incitements

Many emotional incitements which disbalance children and adolescent have no effect on emotionally matured persons. They remain perfectly clam and indifferent towards them.

No Instability in the Expression

During adolescence one gets excited as well as calm very soon. Adolescents lose temper or burst into laughter even on flimsy things. An emotionally mature person is free from this defect.

The entire character of a mature adult is hidden behind his reactions. But this is not the case with an emotionally immature person.

A mature adult exercises self-control over emotional reactions, but an immature one fails in this effort.

A mature adult may show partial reaction also but the immature fellow will either go all out or will not act at all.

Things Necessary for Emotional Maturity

Emotional maturity is a must for achieving success in life. For acquiring emotional maturity one has to struggle against problems of real life. The following things are necessary for attaining emotional maturity.

Good Health

It has been generally observed that one is easily overtaken by emotions when he is tired or ill. Unhealthy persons are easily overtaken by emotions. They have less control over their emotions. Consequently, a person must try to possess sound health to achieve emotional maturity. An adolescent is in the process of maturity from all angles. The effect of health on his development is widely spread. The adolescent should, therefore, try to build good health.

Control over Environment

Total freedom and absolute control, both prove hurdles in the way of acquiring emotional maturity in the case of adolescents. If the environment around the adolescent is in favour of physical and mental development he will then not fail to act rightly while facing a situation and will gradually attain emotional maturity.

Tendency to remain Cheerful

A tendency to remain always cheerful proves an asset in attaining emotional maturity. This tendency lessens one's worries. If this attitude is developed in a person, he will easily attain emotional maturity.

Development of Discretion

During adolescence the development is not complete and the adolescent lacks social experience. So he is often unable to react properly against certain situations. Some persons sometimes get angry over such emotional outburst of an adolescent. If an adolescent is offered opportunities to participate in social activities his power of exercising discretion will increase and this will help in development of his emotional maturity.

Give a Healthy Approach to Emotional Excitement

Despite exercising utmost caution the adolescents sometimes face such a situation which creates emotional tension in them. Not to allow this emotional tension flow out will be harmful. In order to calm it down, the adolescents should be asked to engage themselves in healthy activities. Games and sports, crossword puzzles, and music etc. are activities which are considered healthy. By engaging themselves in healthy activities, the adolescents gradually learn to control their emotions.

SOCIAL MATURITY

Symptoms of Social Maturity

With the development of personality the sphere of acquiring experience also goes on increasing, because the adolescent has to come in contact with various type of persons. If he behaves or reacts to these people according to the social values and situation, he may then be considered to have gained social maturity. A socially mature person will not hesitate like children in leaving the house for residing elsewhere with other persons. Children and adolescents feel greatly perturbed in leaving the home and living with others. They always feel homesick. But in home they desire freedom from elders' control and protest when their actions are criticised. A socially mature person carefully examines the criticism and tries to reform himself accordingly. He wants to do work on his own responsibility. Those adolescents who remain under the strict control of their parents lack self-confidence and therefore acquire social maturity late.

Discharging a Citizen's Obligation a Sign of Social Maturity

Social maturity includes the discharge of civic obligations. A person has not only to discharge his civic duties as a citizen but also has to bring improvement in them. From adolescents one may think that they will not perform their civic duties satisfactorily, but from mature persons adherence to civic values is expected. The more a citizen succeeds in adhering to civic values, the greater respect is accorded to him by the society.

Improved Behaviour towards Friends after Acquiring Social Maturity

A socially matured person is not a blind supporter of his friends like an adolescent. He criticises his friends and does not hide his different opinions. He does whatever he feels proper. He has less regard for friendship before duty.

Personal Interests of No Importance

All this does not mean that a socially mature man has no regard for the interests of others in the society. The matured person may sacrifice his personal interests in the interest of others. Such a person is a brilliant example of social maturity.

MORAL MATURITY

The morality of a socially matured person is not wavering. The matured person always acts on sound principles as far as morality is concerned. He is not wavering like children or adolescent. He has his own values and keeps engaged himself in social activities in accordance with these values. He does not act on others goading. He does whatever he thinks is morally proper. He fully understands the consequences of his actions. He is tolerant and fully aware of human weaknesses. He hates the sin and not the sinner. Whatsoever be the behaviour of the other persons, the socially matured person has full sympathy towards them. In other words, he identifies his own interests with those of the society and tries to effect improvements. The one who is socially immature lacks these virtues. Such a person secretly feels happy over the failure of his friends and also wish them ill.

Morally Mature Person Believes in Gradual Improvement of Society

A morally mature individual certainly wants to bring improvement in his society, but he favours gradual improvement. He does not like to openly criticise vices prevailing in the society. He differs with adolescents in this respect. He is not dejected over failures in his efforts in beginning improvements. He has faith in the gradual improvement of the society.

MENTAL MATURITY

Most of the psychologists believe that a person of average intelligence reaches mental maturity between the age of 13 to 15 years, whereas a person of superior intelligence reaches mental maturity between the age of 16 to 25 years. Mental maturity here means matured thinking or thoughts. Mental maturity may be determined by the following signs :

1. Independent power of decision-making, i.e., making decisions unaffected by the influence of caste, class, tradition, friends or superior officers.
2. To discharge one's responsibilities unaffected by the feeling of good or bad.
3. Considering calmly the merits and demerits of the case unaffected by emotions.
4. Reaching a right decision even before seeing the situation.
5. Solving problems on "give and take" basis and not forgetting the consequences in enthusiasm.
6. Remain courteous.

Mental Maturity helps Maturity of Aptitudes and Stability of Ideals

An individual develops maturity of aptitude with mental maturity. He sticks to his aptitude and ideals unlike children and adolescents. The aptitudes take a permanent footing. His wavering in respect of tastes and trades disappears. Maturity of taste develops after maturity of mind. This is Strang's observation. According to him, tastes stabilise between the age of 25 and 55. According to Bele, a mentally matured person does not change his view on current national and international problems easily. He is not influenced by publicity in forming his opinion on problems. He depends on his knowledge and experience in forming an opinion.

Mental Maturity Destroys Blind Faith

Mental maturity destroys blind faith. Many actions of children and adolescents are based on blind faith but mental maturity drives away blind faith. Consequently, children are more susceptible to blind faith as compared to adolescents and adolescents more susceptible as compared to adults. Science also helps in removing blind faith which is mostly related to fortune, natural objects and some animals. People, for example, consider it a bad omen if a black cat passes across the road in front of a walking person. Similarly, people consider it a good omen if they see a fish while going on an assignment. All this is due to blind faith. Everyone concerned with the development of a child's or adolescent's personality should try to him free of blind beliefs.

Mental Maturity Helps Develop Power of Self-Introspection

An individual develops power of self-introspection with the attainment of mental maturity. He is then able to realise what is good or bad for him. There is no doubt that it is difficult for one to realise his own shortcomings. However, when one gains this power he reaches the climax of mental maturity. The power of self-introspection is, therefore, not only the climax of mental maturity but also the climax of the development of humanity. We have to help children and adults to reach this stage. The children mostly accept the advice tendered to them since their mental development is comparatively less but adolescent accept the advice after much reservations. They occasionally become critical of the advice given to them. Needless to remark that utmost care should be taken in dealing with them.

SUMMARY

With the development of maturity, interests, aptitudes, notions and abilities also mature. A mature person can act on his own responsibility. Age alone is not related with maturity. A person of 50 or 60 may be less mature than a adolescent in certain aspects. Development of maturity is closely associated with the development of good social virtues and values. The modern man is less physically mature than his forefathers in ancient days. This is because of the impact of the evil results, and sophisticated living in the highly industrialized society of today. A mature person feels freedom and fearlessness in undertaking a responsibility. Maturity may be of various types, such as, physical, emotional, social, moral and mental. These various types of maturity do not come at the same time. Their development is gradual and interrelated also. It is the responsibility of elders to see that the various types of maturity develop in a desirable manner within a reasonable period of growth.

Exercises

1. Define maturity and explain its various aspects with concrete illustrations.
2. How has the modern civilization influenced the development of various type of maturities ? Explain with some examples.
3. Describe the symptoms of emotional maturity.
4. What are the signs of social maturity?

Notes

1. Doll, E.A., 'Social Maturation', Proc. 5th Ins. Except, Child, *Child Res. Clin.* 31-26, 1938.

Bibliography

Abernethy, M.E. : Correlations in physical and mental growth, *Educ. Psychol.*, 16, 1925, 458-466, 439-546.

Ackerson, L : *Children's behaviour problems,* Chicago Univ. Press, Chicago, 1931, 109-121, 249-261.

Adler, A. : *Study of Organ inferiority and its psychical compensations,* The Nervous and Mental Disease Publishing Company, New York, 1917.

Anderson, H.H. : An examination of the concepts of domination and integration in relation to dominance and ascendance, *Psychgol. Rev.* 47, 1940, 21-37.

Anderson, J.P. : A study of the relationship between certain aspect of parental behaviour and atitudes and the behaviour of junior high School pupils., *Teach. Coll. Contr. Educ.*, No. 809, 1940.

Arlitt, A.H., *Adolescent Psychology.*, New York, American Book Company, 1933.

Austin, F.M., An analysis of the motives of adolescents for the choice of the teaching profession, *Brit. F. Educ. Psychol,* 1, 1931, 87-103.

Baber, R.E., Marriage and the Family, McGrew. Hill, New York, 1939.

Baldwin, B.T. : The physical growth of children from birth to maturity *Univ Ia Stud. Child Welf.* 1, No. 1, 1921.

— —, : The determination of sex maturation in boys by a laboratory method. *J. Comp. Psychol.* 8, 1928, 39-43.

Barr, E.D. : A psychological analysis of fashion motivation, *Arch Psychol,* N.Y., Vol. 171, 1934.

Bartlett, E.R. & Harris, D.B., Personality factors in delinquency, *Sch. & Soc.*, 43, 1937, 453-656.

Bayley, N. : Size and body build of adolescents in relation to rate of skeletal maturing, *Child Development,* 14, 1943, 51-89.

Bell, H. M., *Youth Tell Their Story,* American Council on Education, Washingtion, D.C. 1938.

— —, : *The Theory and Practice of Counseling.*, Stanford Univ. Calif, Stanford Univ. Press, 1939.

Blos, P., : *The Adolescent Personality.*, Appleton Century, New York, 1941.

Blumer, H., *Movies and Conduct*, Macmillan, New York, 1933.

Bonner, A., Adolecent anxieties, *Child Stud.*, 13, 206-208.

Brill, A. A. *Fundamental Conceptions of Psycho-analysis*, Har Court Brace, New York, 1921.

Brown, M., Leadership among high school pupils, *Teach. Coll. Contr. Educ.*, No. 559, 1933.

Buhler, C., *Das Seelenleben der Fngendlichen*— Wien : Gustav Fischer, 1927.

Burgess, E. W., *The Adolesceat in the Family*, Appleton-Cenbtury, New York, 1934.

Burt, C., *The Young Delinquent.*, Appleton-Century, New York, 1925.

Butterfield, O. M., Love problems of adolescence, *Teach Coll. Contr. Educ*, No. 768, 1939.

Carey, T. F., *The Relation of Physical Growth to Develop Mental Age in Boys*, The Catholic Univ. of America Press, Washington, 1935.

Carter, W. P., *The Only Child in the Family*, The Univ. of Chicago Libraries., Chicago, 1940.

Cason, H., Common Annoyances *Psychol. Monogr*, No. 2, 1930.

Chadwick, M., *Adolescent Girlhool*, Fohn Day, New York, 1932.

Chaube, S. P., *Bal Manovigyan*, Ram Narain Lal, Allahabad, 1950.

Cole, L., *Psychgology of Adolescence*, Rinehart, Rev. Ed., New York, 1942.

— —, *Attaining Maturity*, Rinehart, New York, 1944.

Conklin, E.S., *Principles of Adolescent Psychology*, Holt, New York, 1933.

— —, *Childhood and adolescene*. In Skinner, C.E., *Educational Psy., Chap.* 11, Prentice Hall, New York, 1936.

Dale, E., *Children's Attendance at Nation Pictures*, Macmillan, New York, 1933.

Dimock, H. S., *Rediscovering the Adolescent*, Association Press, New York, 1937.

Doll, E. A., Social maturation, *Proc, 5th inst. Except, Child. Child Res. Clin*, 1938, 31-36.

Fleege, U. H., *Self revelation of the Adolescent Boy*, Bruce Pub, Milwaukee, 1945.

Fleming, C. M., *Adolescence*, Routledgeand Kegan Paul Ltd., London, 1948.

Fleming, E. G., Pleasing Personality, *J. Soc Psychol*, 3, 1932, 100-107.

— —, : A factor analysis of the personality of high-school leaders, *J. Appl. Psychol.* 19, 1935, 596-605.

Folsom, J. K., *The Family,* Wiley, New York, 1934.

Forman, H. J., *Our Movie Made Children*, Macmillan, New York, 1935.

Freud, S., *A General Introduction to Psychonalysis*, Boni and Liveright, New York, 1920.

Furfey, P. H., *The Gang Age*. Macmillan, New York, 1926.

Gates, G. S., An observational study of anger, *J. Exp. Psychol*, 9, 1926, 325-336.

Goodenough, F. L. *Developmental Psychology*, Appleton-Century, 2nd Ed., New York, 1945.

Gray, J. S., *Psychology in Human Affairs*, McGraw-Hill, New York, 1946.

Green, G. H., *The Daydream*, University of London Press Ltd., 1923.

Guetzkow, H.H., and Bowman. P. H., *Man and Hunger*, Bre-thern Pub. House, Elgin III, 1946.

Hall, G. S., *Adolescence*, Appleton-Century, New York, 1904.

Hamilton, G. V., *A Research in Marriage*, Boni, New York, 1929.

Hardy, M. C., Adjustment scores of adolescents having history of frequent illness during childhood, *Amer, J. Ortho*, 7, 1937, 204-209.

Hart, F. W., *Teachers and Teaching*., Macmillan, New York, 1934.

Hartshorne, H. and May, M., *Studies in Deceit*, Macmillan, New York, 1928.

Hartshorne, H., May. M., and Shuttleworth, F. K., *Studies in the Nature of Character*. 3 Vols., Macmillan, New York, 1930.

Havighurst, R. J. and Taba, Hilda, *Adolescent Character and Personality*, John Wiley, New York, 1949.

Healy, W., *The Individual Delinquent,* Little, Brown, Boston, 1915.

Healy, W., and Bronner, A. F., *Delinquent and Criminals*, Macmillan, New York, 1928.

— —, New light on delinquency and its treatment, Yale Univ. Press, New Heven, 1936.

Hetzer, H., Der Einlluss der negativen Phase and Soziales Verhalten and Literarischeproduktion pubertierender madchen, *Quellen and Studies*, 5, 1926 1-143.

— —, Systematische Dauerbeobachtungen and Jugedlichen uberden Verlauf der negativen Phase, *Zeitsch. F Padogog. Psychol. u. Experim Podogog*, 28, 1927, 80-96.

Hicks, J. A., and Hayes, M., Study of the characteristics of 250 Junior high school children, *Child Dev*. 9, 1938, 219-242.

Hildreth, G., Adolescent interests and abilities. *J. Genet, Psychol*, 1933, 379-393.

Hollingworth, L.S., *Gifted Children : There Nature and Nurture*, Macmillan, New York, 1920.

— —, *The Psychology of Adolescence,* Appleton-Century, New York, 1928.

— —, Adolescent child, *In* Murchison, C. A., *A Handbook of Child Psychology*, 2nd Ed., The Clark Univ Press, Worester, Mass, 1933, pp. 882-908.

Hoskins, R. G., *The Tides of Life*, Norton, New York, 1933.

Hunter, E. C. and Jordon, A. M., An analysis of qualities associated with leadership among college students, *J. Educ. Psychol*, 30, 1939, 497-509.

Hurlock, E. B., Motivation in fashion, *Arch Psychol*, No. 111, New York, 1929.

— —, *Adolescent Development*, McGraw-Hill, New York, 1949.

— —, *Child Development*, McGraw-Hill, New York, 1950.

Jones, H. E., *Development in Adolescence*. Appleton-Century, New York, 1943.

Jones, M. C., Guiding the Adolescent, *Prog. Educ*, 15, 605-609.

— —, Adolescence. In Monroe, W. S., *Encyclopaedia of Educational Research*, Macmillan, New York, 1941, 179-182.

(See also pp. 168-171 for "Moral Concepts and conduct" by-Jones, V).

Jordon, A. M., *Children's Interest in Reading,* Univ. of North Carolina Press, Chapel Hill, N. C., 1926.

Katz, D. and Allport, F. H., *Students' Attitudes*, The Craftsman Press, Syracuse, N. Y., 1931.

Kupky, O., *The Religious Development of Adolescents,* Macmillan, New York, 1928.

Landis, Cetal, *Sex in Development,* Hoeber, New York, 1940.

Leal, M. A., *Physiological Maturity in Relation to certain Characteristics of Boys and Girls*, University of Pennsylvania, Philadelphia, 1929.

Lehman, H. C. and Witty, P. A., Sex difference in vocational attitutdes, *F Appl Psychal,* 20, 1936, 586-585.

— —, *The Psychology of Play Activities*, H. S. Barnes & Co., New York, 1927.

Link, H. C., *The Return of Religion*, Macmillan, New York, 1937.

Lockhart, E. G., *Improving Your Personality*, Walton Pub. Co. Chicago, 1929.

Lund, F. H., *Emotions : Their Psychological, and educative Implications*, Ronald, New York, 1939.

Meltzr, H., Students adjustment in anger, *F. Soc. Psych*, 4, 1933, 285, 308.

— —, Anger adjustment in relation to intelligence and achievement, *F. Genet, Psych*, 5, 1937, 63-32.

Mckinney, F., *Psychology of Personal Adjustment*, Willy, New York, 1941.

McLaughlin, Sister M. A., The genesis and constancy of ascendence and submission as personality traits, *Univ. in Stud. Educ*, 6, No. 5, 1930.

Moore, H. T., Laboratory tests of anger, fear and sex interest, *Amer, F. Psychology*, 28, 1919, 390-395.

Partridge, E. D., *Social Psychology*, Prentice-Hall, New York, 1938.

Pigors, F., Type of folloewrs, *F. Social Psychol*, 5, 1934, 378-383.

Pressey, S. L. and Robinson, F. P., *Psychology and the New Education*, Harper, New York, 1944.

Reynolds, F. J., Factors of leadership among senior of Central High School. *J. Edu, Res.* 37, 356-361, Tulsa, Oklahoma.

Rockwood, L. D. and Ford, M. E. N., *Youth, Marriage and Parenthood*, Wiley, New York, 1945.

Rogers, R. H. and Austin, O. L., Intelligence quotients of juvenile delinquent, *J. Juv.*, Res., 81, 103-106.

Rothney, J. W. M., Interests of public secondary school boys., *J. Educ, Psychol*, 28, 1937, 561-590.

Sakellariou, G., Anxieties and complexes of greek youth, *Psychol. Abstr*, 14, No. 621, 1940.

Scheinfeld, A., *Women and Men*, Harcourt, Brace, New Yerk, 1943.

Spaulding, C. B., Types of Junior-college leaders, *Social and Soc. Res.* 18, 1933, 164, 168.

Stagner, R., *Psychology of Personality*, MacGraw-Hill, New York, 1948.

Stern, W., *Psychology of Early Childhood*, Holt, New York, 1930.

Stevens, G. C., Autobiographical material concerning the childhood environments and the effects on the after adjustments of 100 recidivlsts and 100 college freshmen., *Amer J. Ortho*, 2, 1932, 279-303.

Stoddard, L., *The Story of Youth,* Cosmopoliton Book Corporation, New York, 1938.

Stoltz, H. R. Jones, M. C., & Chaffey, J., The junior high school age, *Univ. High School, F. Calif,* 15, 1937, 63-72.

Stoltz, H. R.& Stoltz, L. M., Adolescent problems related to Semantic variations, *43rd Yearb, Nat, Soc, Stud, Educ.* 1944, pp. 3099.

Stott, L. H., Personality development in farm, small town and city children, *Univ, Nebr. Agric, Expr, Station,* Res. Bull, No. 114, 1939.

Strang, R., Guidance in personality development, *37th Yearb. Nat. Soc. Stud Educ*, pp. 179-228.

Stratton, G. M., Emotions and the incidence of disease, *J. Abnorm, Soc, Psychol,* 21,1927, 19-23.

Strong, E. K., *Change in Interest with Age*, Stanford Univ. Calif, Stanford Univ., 1931.

— —, Interest maturity, *Person J.* 12, 1933, 77-90.

Sullenger, T. E., Extracurricular leisure time activities. *Recreation*, 32, 1938, 509-510.

Sward, K., Temperament and religious experience, *J. Abnorm. Soc, Psychol.*, 4, 1933, 406-429.

Symonds, P. M., Life problems and interests of adolescents, *Sch. Rev,* 44, 1936, 506-518.

— —, *The Psychology of Parent-child Relationships*, Appleton-Century, New York, 1939.

Taylor, K. W., *Do Adolescents need Parents* ? Appleton-Century, New York, 1942.

Tead, O., *The Art of Leadership*, Whittlesey House, McGraw-Hill, New York, 1936.

Terman, L. M., *Genetic Study of Genius*, Standford Univ, Calif, Stanford Univ. p. 1925, Vol. 1., 1926, Vol. 2, 1930, Vol. 3.

Terman, L. M. & Lime, M., *Children's Reading,* Appleton-Century, New York, 1927.

— —, *The Gang,* 2nd ed, Univ. of Chicago Pess., Chicago, 1936.

Torrance, P., The Influence of the broken home on adolescent adjustment, *F. Educ. Social.* 18, 1945, 356-364.

Varendonck, *J. The Psychology of Day-dreams,* Macmillan, New York, 1921.

Vecerka, J., Das soziale Verhalten von Madchen wahrend dar Reifezeit. *Quellen u. Stud*, 4, 1936, 49-121.

Wang, C. K. A., The significance of early personal history for certain personality traits. *Amer. J. Psychol.*, 44, 1932, 768–774.

Watson, *Psychology from the Standpoint of Behaviourist*. Chap. 11.

Whitley, M. T., Children's interest in collecting, *J. Educ, Psychol*, 20, 1929, 249-261.

Williams, F. E., *Adolescence*, Rinehart, New York, 1920.

Witty, P. A., & Lehman, H. G., Further studies of children's interest in collecting, *J. Educ., Psychol.* 21, 1930, 112–127.

Woodworth, R.S. & Morquis, D.G., *Psychology*, 5th ed. Holt, New York, 1947.

Wren, C. G. & Harley, D. L., *Time on their Hands : A Report on Leisure, Recreation, and Young People*, American Council on Education, Washington D. C., 1941.

Zachry, C. B., *Emotion and Conduct in Adolescene*. Appleton-Century, 1940.

INDEX